IDEAL MAN IN
CLASSICAL SOCIOLOGY

IDEAL MAN IN
CLASSICAL SOCIOLOGY

The Views of Comte, Durkheim, Pareto, and Weber

Peter Roche de Coppens

THE PENNSYLVANIA STATE UNIVERSITY PRESS
UNIVERSITY PARK AND LONDON

Library of Congress Cataloging in Publication Data

De Coppens, Peter Roche, 1938-
    Ideal man in classicial sociology.

    Bibliography: p. 161
    Includes index.
    1. Sociology—Methodology.   2. Sociology—
History.   3. Man.   I. Title.
HM24.D38   301'.01   75-27174
ISBN 0-271-01206-4

CONTENTS

PREFACE

This inquiry into the relationship, between consciousness and existence, between the scholar ideals and life work, as reflected in sociological theory, is in part a sequel to my exploratory study of the relationship between self-image and *Weltanschauung* completed at Columbia University in 1964 under the title "Spiritual Man in the Modern World," but it is also in part a new and autonomous development.

Although I owe much to many for the conception of the present investigation, I am particularly indebted to Dr. Werner Stark for suggesting the application of my "quest for ideal man" notion to a review of the lives and works of the founders of modern sociology. Throughout the writing of this book Professor Stark was a patient guide and source of inspiration. His works, teachings, and personal example embody—in my mind—the best of the great humanistic tradition in contemporary sociology.

I am also indebted to Professors Joseph Fitzpatrick, Charles Serei, and my other teachers at Fordham University, and to my many students, there and elsewhere, who have helped me to clarify and develop the ideas guiding this study. I am grateful to Miss Joan T. O'Connor for her companionship, suggestions, and corrections in editing the final text. Finally, I am grateful to the Woodrow Wilson Foundation for a fellowship that enabled me to work full time on this book and to travel near and far to gather the necessary materials.

The translations of all sources not published in English were done by me. The bibliography is selected; it includes only works quoted directly or central to my research. A great many other books were influential in a secondary way.

The seminal ideas of this book did not begin with this inquiry and will not terminate with it. It is my intention to continue this investigation, and I hope my work will inspire other scholars to continue and branch off where I stopped.

1

BACKGROUND ASSUMPTIONS

Human Nature and the
Concept of Ideal Man

The central aim of this book is to contribute further understanding of how social theories and methodologies have come into being as the products of given sociocultural milieus and intellectual climates, as well as of human genius and creativity. Key concepts and basic orientations of social theories and methodologies are subconsciously, preconsciously, and consciously influenced by one central concept: the concept of the ideal man held by their authors. The basic assumption here is that every social theorist does have, explicitly or implicitly, a conception of the ideal man—of the good, fully actualized man—which he will strive to embody in his life and work, and which he hopes his life and work will help others to realize.

My major hypothesis is that such a conception of the ideal man, embedded within and arising from the author's theory of human nature, emerging from his crucial existential experiences in a given sociocultural milieu with a particular Zeitgeist, does have a profound and comprehensive effect on both the kinds of questions he will ask and the way in which he will answer them, that is, on the formation and orientation of his social theory. To develop and support this hypothesis, I have selected four major classical social theorists who contributed to the theoretical and methodological foundations of modern sociology: Auguste Comte, Emile Durkheim, Vilfredo Pareto, and Max Weber.

I try to show how each of these social theorists did have a conception of an ideal man; how this conception emerged from their personal lives and experiences in the sociocultural milieu in which they lived; and how it significantly affected their social theories and methodologies. In so doing, I hope to prove my hypothesis and to make a valid contribution both to the understanding of the nature, genesis, limitations, and structuring elements of social theory, and to the sociology of knowledge. Thus, I shall begin each investigation by presenting a brief biographical sketch of the theorist and a brief outline of the sociocultural milieu in which he lived and worked. Then, I shall delineate and analyze his theory of human nature and his resultant conception of the ideal man. Finally, I shall show how this conception profoundly affected both his intellectual system—his social theories and methodologies—and the course of his life and work.

At the core of the Western intellectual tradition lies the Delphic injunction "know thyself," an injunction standing as the universal axis upon which people of all times and places, of all races and levels of human consciousness, have begun to build the edifice of their human knowledge and philosophy of life. It stands at the center of the quest for truth and self-realization; men of all times correctly intuited that, unless they knew and understood themselves as the medium through which knowledge flowed and unfolded, and unless they understood their own nature, limits, and potentialities, they could not obtain knowledge about, or formulate an objective perspective of, the universe in which they lived.

Today we, too, have an urge to know and to understand ourselves, and, thus, the ancient and eternal quest has been preserved and transmitted by the humanistic tradition. The modern social sciences, particularly after World War II, with psychology and sociology developing new and more complex theories and methodologies, have begun to reexamine the central assumptions and the major aims of the humanistic tradition, seeking to be under its ideological umbrella. And it is to the broader understanding of the key assumptions of these theories and methodologies, of their construction, and of their fundamental implications for man and society that this book is aiming with concrete examples and a model drawn from the life and work of four classical social theorists.

Social theories constitute one of the three major forms that the quest for truth and self-realization assumed historically: the study of man's relation to man—the investigation of the nature, causes, and consequences of human interaction (the other two being the study of man's relation to God and of man's relation to nature). Social theories, on the whole, have two major aims. They describe and explain why human relations are what they are: how man is transformed from a biopsychic organism into a social and rational being; the genesis and the mechanisms by which man's psychosocial nature unfolds and expresses itself; how human societies can exist and why they change; the specific structures and functions of the major social institutions of a given society, and the processes by which they transform themselves. In addition, social theories somehow help man actualize his latent human potentialities and faculties to the fullest possible extent by improving and perfecting his being and life in the society in which he lives. As Alvin Gouldner perceptively writes:

> All social theories, in my view, embody the traces of *social diagnosis* and *social therapy*. They are never simply disinterested efforts to describe and explain social reality. One way in which social theories can be understood, then, is as analysis, clear or cryptic, of the cause and possible cures of the ills of the society to which the theorist has been subjected.[1]

As such, social theories are not merely descriptive and analytical studies of *what is*, they are also, consciously or unconsciously and more or less explicitly, explanatory and evaluative investigations of what *ought to be*. In other words, each contains and projects some value judgment, some ideal of its author.

> All social theories, however technical and esoteric, bear the trace marks of some judgment about the social world; all reflect a vision, however dim and indistinct, of a world more desirable than the one the theorist knows. To be a social theorist is not simply to seek out the world that is; it is also to reach for a world that might be, even if this is done with pick-pocket fingers. To be a social theorist is not simply to describe and analyze the world that is; it is also to pronounce a judgment on it, even if this is done in a ventriloquist's voice. To be a social theorist is to be the oedipal heir to shamans and priests and to conjurers of philosopher-kings. It is to be a maker and shaker of worlds that are and of worlds that might be. . . . All social theories involve some diagnosis of human problems and all embody some therapy for them.[2]

If social theories are not merely a diagnosis of what is and of why certain social conditions prevail in a given sociocultural milieu, but also a cure and a blueprint for what could be and what ought to be, they must be anchored in judgments derived from a vision which is based on certain ideals. As Gouldner rightly claims: "Underneath the generalizations of formal social theory there is always a concrete image of a specific, good society."[3] Gouldner, in other words, claims that within the infrastructure of all social theory there lurks, consciously or subconsciously, the ideal of a good society. But I contend that within the infrastructure of social theory there lies hidden not only the ideal of a good society but also the ideal of a good man and, in some cases, a conception of God, or a supreme reality. I also claim that the ideal of a good society depends on and emerges from the conception of the ideal man I intend to explore in the social theories of Comte, Durkheim, Pareto, and Weber.

Gouldner, in his recent work, *The Coming Crisis in Western Sociology,* clearly intuited the central hypothesis of the present inquiry, but did not fully explore it.

> Like it or not, and know it or not, sociologists will organize their researches in terms of their prior assumptions; the character of sociology will depend upon them and will change when they change. To explore the character of sociology, to know what a sociology is, therefore, requires us to identify its deepest assumptions about man and society. For these reasons it will not be to its methods of study to which I will look for an understanding of its character, but rather to its assumptions about man and society. . . .
>
> Deliberately formulated social theories . . . contain at least two distinguishable elements. One element is the explicitly formulated assumptions, which may be called "postulations." But they contain a good deal more. They also contain a second set of assumptions that are unpostulated and unlabeled, and these I will term "background assumptions." I will call them background assumptions because, on the one hand, they provide the background out of which the postulations in part emerge and, on the other hand, not being expressly formulated, they remain in the background of the theorist's attention.[4]

Gouldner claims, therefore, as I do, that the work and orientation of social thinkers, as well as that of other thinkers, is affected by a "subtheoretical" and axiological set of metaphysical beliefs that are formed prior to and independent of their scientific endeavors; and that these metaphysical beliefs and ideals are "often internalized in us long before the intellectual age of consent. They are affectively-laden cognitive tools that are developed early in the course of our socialization into a particular culture and are built deeply into our character structures."[5]

Gouldner, therefore, shares one of the basic conclusions of the present book: in studying the society in which he lives and in seeking to understand it, the social theorist is seeking to understand himself and to comprehend the causes and consequences of his many existential experiences—that social knowledge is colored by self-knowledge and leads to it. The analysis and theoretical explanation of this book will essentially focus, however, on one of the assumptions that I consider crucial: the theorist's conception of the ideal man, which is assumed to play a significant role in the development and orientation of his social theories and methodological approaches.

Turning from a general consideration of the structural development and orientation of social theory to a specific field—the sociology of knowledge—which can be applied to understand the general, I found that within the sociology of knowledge there are several approaches and hermeneutic perspectives which illumine and explain the theoretical roots and the axiological foundations of social theories. Basically, there are two: the theory of ideology and the theory of the social determination of thought, which constitute the polar axes of the modern sociology of knowledge. As Werner Stark sees it:

> In the past, two rather disparate, nay irreconcilable, preoccupations have coexisted within the sociology of knowledge and constantly cut across each other: the study of the political element in thought, of what is commonly called "ideology," and the investigation of the social element in thinking, the influence of the social groundwork of life on the formation of a determinate mental image of reality. The one has sought to lay bare hidden factors which turn us away from the truth, the other to identify forces which tend to impart a definite direction to our search for it.[6]

The central thesis of the sociology of knowledge, in its present level of theoretical and empirical development, has been incisively captured by Stark in the following words:

> [The sociology of knowledge] insists that the individual himself cannot be understood unless he is seen in his social setting, in the living interplay of the self with other selves. It claims that, if we want to comprehend the full meaning of any cultural phenomenon, we must go beyond it and study the social circumstances with which it is genetically connected. . . . Its ultimate aim is both a doctrine and a method: a doctrine or theory which will show exactly what the interrelations of social substructure and intellectual superstructure are.[7]

This fledgling discipline within the growing field of modern sociology, at least in the tradition developed by Kant, Rickert, Scheler, Weber, and Stark, is based on two fundamental insights which constitute its major contribution and teaching:

That human thought and social existence form an organic unity so that the first, issuing from and being shaped by the second, can be correctly explained and properly understood only within the perspective of the second. Here, therefore, social existence is conceived as the determining factor, within certain limits imposed by the freedom and spontaneity of the human spirit, of human consciousness and its various creations and constructions.

Hence, that the personality, the work, and the philosophy of any theorist, or any sociocultural phenomenon, for that matter, can be truly captured and understood in depth only through the total life situation of that individual or phenomenon embedded within the context of its total sociocultural and historical situation.

Karl Mannheim conceived the theory of ideology as operating, basically, at two levels, "political ideology" and "utopian strivings," and he linked, erroneously in my opinion, the social determination of thought to a panideological assumption.

> In principle it was politics which first discovered the sociological method in the study of intellectual phenomena. Basically it was in political struggles that for the first time men became aware of the unconscious collective motivations which had always guided the direction of thought. Political discussion is, from the very first, more than theoretical argumentation; it is the tearing off of disguises—the unmasking of those unconscious motives which bind the group existence to its cultural aspirations and its theoretical arguments. . . .
>
> The concept of "ideology" reflects the one discovery which emerged from political conflict, namely, that ruling groups can in their thinking become so intensively interest-bound to a situation that they are simply no longer able to see certain facts which would undermine their sense of domination. There is implicit in the word "ideology" the insight that in certain situations the collective unconscious of certain groups obscures the real condition of society both to itself and to others and thereby stabilizes it.
>
> The concept of utopian thinking reflects the opposite discovery of the political struggle, namely that certain oppressed groups are intellectually so strongly interested in the destruction and transformation of a given situation of society that they unwittingly see only those elements in the situation which tend to negate it. Their thinking is incapable of correctly diagnosing an existing condition of society. They are not at all concerned with what really exists. Their thought is never a diagnosis of the situation; it can be

used only as a direction for action. In the utopian mentality, the collective unconscious, guided by wishful representation and the will to action, hides certain aspects of reality. It turns its back on everything which would shake its belief or paralyse its desire to change things.[8]

Stark, on the other hand, recognizes that a genuine sociology of knowledge is possible and that a social determination of human thinking can bypass the Scylla and Charybdis of ideological and utopian distortions and thus proceed toward an objective, even though relative, description and analysis of the investigated social reality.

> The thesis of the sociology of knowledge is that the choice of the vantage point from which the *ens universale* is envisaged depends in every concrete society on the human relationships which make that society what it is; but it is not asserted that selfish or sectional interests enter into the matter already at the point where the fundamental vision springs into being. . . . The sociology of knowledge does not deal with warped thought; rather it deals with the crystallization or "concretization" of thought. . . . The sociology of knowledge deals with the formation of a specific world view, the doctrine of ideology with its deformation; the former is concerned with a positive, the latter with a negative phenomenon.[9]

At the root of both ideological and socially determined thought, Stark sees certain values or value facts. But, although in the former case these values are psychologically derived and unconscious, in the latter they are both psychologically and socially derived and unconscious.

> [The difference between ideological and socially determined thinking] does not consist in the fact that ideological thought is value-bound and socially determined thought is value-free. Value-free thinking may be an ideal, but it is certainly nowhere a reality. . . . It lies in the fact that the valuations at the root of ideologies are only psychologically subliminal, whereas the valuations at the basis of socially determined ideas are both psychologically and socially subliminal. . . . Ideological thought is determined by a striving for what ought to be and hence is not; whereas socially determined thought is determined by a recognition of that which is. . . . Both ideological and socially determined thought are based on antecedently conceived value-systems, but

whereas the values behind ideologies are values yet to be realized, values still in the air, the values behind socially determined thought are values already realized, values that have come down to earth, value incarnate—in a word, as the philosophers have it, value-facts.[10]

Mannheim is correct when he says, "in studying what is, we cannot totally rule out what ought to be. In human life, the motives and ends of action are part of the process by which action is achieved and are essential in seeing the relation of the parts to the whole. Without the end most acts would have no meaning and no interest to us";[11] and "without evaluative conceptions, without the minimum of a meaningful goal, we can do nothing in either the sphere of the social or the sphere of the psychic."[12] I also agree with Stark's assessment of the social a priori, the axiological system, which is the value system of the society in which the seeker after truth lives. Thus the prior valuations with which he works and which enable him to do his work are not prejudices or value judgments. They are the value facts that stand at the basis of the society in which he lives and which have shaped his mind both for practical conduct and for theoretical contemplation. Values, therefore, can be seen as maneuvering a person into a certain existential position and not as falsifying his vision. He can speak the truth as he sees it for it will be the objective truth *in his situation.*[13]

My specific aim in this study is to show the existence of a conception of an ideal man behind every serious social theory, influencing and orienting the theory at an infrastructural and axiological as well as at a structural level. To do so, it is necessary to first outline the basic noological framework of social theory and locate therein the place and the structuring impact of such a conception.

I have come to the conclusion that social theory rests implicitly or explicitly on four basic sets of interrelated assumptions, or perspectives:

1. *A theory of human nature,* or a basic set of assumptions dealing with what man is, and how he became what he is; it concerns what man can know and how he knows, as well as how man can fully actualize his human potentialities in terms of a conception of an ideal man.

2. *A theory of human society,* or a basic set of assumptions dealing with what society is, how it became what it is, and how it functions; it concerns the relationship between the sociocultural forces of society and the psychosocial forces of the individual, as well as what society can and should become.

3. *A theory of the nature of history,* or a basic set of assumptions dealing with the biography of man and society, with the evolutionary perspective that has shaped the present sociocultural and psychosocial forces and processes; it concerns the concrete biography of the unfoldment of human consciousness, the articulation of sociocultural perspectives, and the agents of social change and integration.
4. *A theory of the nature, scope, and purpose of sociology,* or a set of assumptions forming a basic conception of what sociology is and of the nature, scope, and purpose of its theories and methodologies.

The most important of these four basic sets of interrelated assumptions is the first, the theory of human nature. This theory, which contains implicitly two classical injunctions of Greek philosophy: "know thyself" and "man, realize thyself, become thy higher self," includes as its major components a conception of man, a conception of human knowledge, and a conception of the ideal man which, together, form an interrelated whole. It involves, furthermore, both a theoretical part and a practical part, an expansion of human consciousness, of human knowledge and understanding and an actualization and realization of man's essence and potentialities.

Man is that peculiar being who is both something today and who becomes something else tomorrow; he is not a finished and complete being, rather, he is a being-in-the-making, a being who is undergoing an evolution, which, with the passage of time, becomes more and more a conscious evolution, an evolution in which man deliberately makes himself and forges his destiny by his efforts and ideals.

What man is today is determined by what man was and did in the past—the sum total of what happened to him in the past in the light of his nature and potentialities—and by what man strives to become and to accomplish in the future. The blueprint for this is beautifully embodied in his ideals, chief among which is his conception of the ideal man.

Man's behavior, his strivings and creations, are determined not only by his past but also by his future, by what he hopes to become and strives to achieve. Human behavior and human creations cannot be explained mechanistically; they must also be explained teleologically.

Only by combining the mechanistic approach (materialistic, past-oriented) and the teleological approach (psychosocial, future-oriented) can a satisfactory model be provided for man's doings and expressions. Man is both a pleasure-driven animal and a goal-oriented being; he has to cope with survival, physical adaptation, and psychosocial adjustment, but he also seeks to realize, objectify, and personify ideals.

Either aspect of his being can function as the unifying and integrating principle of his personality and thus act as the determining factor of his behavior. In mentally creative persons, moreover, and particularly in social and religious prophets, the realization and personification of ideals is the key factor.

The theory of the nature of society, ultimately, is the externalization, projection, and manifestation of the fundamental traits and drives of man's nature in a social context. Thus, the nature and dynamics of the social bond are underpinned, consciously or unconsciously, by the theory of human nature. Furthermore, the theory of society, like that of the nature of man, aims at describing and analyzing both what society is and what society can and should eventually become. Thus it embodies an ideal for the good society and the good life just as the theory of human nature embodies an ideal for the good man. Theories of the nature of society indicate how human nature expresses and realizes itself within a sociocultural context which depends infrastructurally and axiologically on an implicit or explicit conception of the ideal man.

The theory of the nature of history is, ultimately, the biography of the expression, unfoldment, and actualization of key traits, drives, and dispositions of human nature; it shows human nature expressing and realizing itself within a sociocultural context seen through time. Theories of the nature of history indicate, perhaps better than any other approach, how human potentialities and faculties develop and actualize themselves in various types of concrete historical expressions. They contain and show the laws of being and becoming of the individual and of social organization. And, as such, they, too, are infrastructurally and axiologically dependent upon an implicit or explicit conception of the ideal man.

Finally, the theory of social science—the basic conception of the nature, scope, and purpose of sociology—is a theory of human cognition, developed and systematized by certain assumptions and operationalized through other assumptions and procedures. It is the set of assumptions and means by which human nature can be studied and investigated in its individual and collective expressions, as it appears at one time, as well as through time, in its evolution. Thus it is structurally dependent on a theory of human nature and, infrastructurally and axiologically, on a conception of the ideal man.

From the foregoing, it is clear that these four "theories" form an organic unity in which all the parts are mutually related and interact. They rest on and "feed back" into the first, the theory of human nature with its three conceptions of man, of human knowledge, and of the ideal man.

In the eighteenth and, later, in the nineteenth century, the nature of man was studied more and more in empirical terms, that is, in terms of what could be seen, directly observed, reasoned, and experienced; it was studied less and less in terms of "authorities," "revelations," and religious dogmas.

To know oneself and to understand human nature with its limits and potentialities, educated minds turned toward biology and psychology, and, later, toward sociology and anthropology. Some also turned toward history and philosophy. Thus, society became a mirror for man, a great chart for studying the expressions and manifestations of the countless traits and dispositions of human nature in action. History became the panorama of the unfolding of human nature performing countless experiments and developing innumerable avenues for self-expression and self-realization.

To articulate the conception of the ideal man that stands behind a given social theory, at its infrastructural and axiological level proves to be a worthwhile and theoretically rewarding endeavor; it yields a key variable for developing an explanatory model for the understanding of the genesis, unfoldment, and orientation of social theory. This is what I shall attempt to do in this book with an analysis of the social thought and of the intellectual systems of four selected theorists. As such, it is my hope to make a significant contribution to the understanding of the structure, infrastructure, and axiological foundation of social theory and to the further development of the sociology of knowledge.

2

AUGUSTE COMTE

The Man, His Work, and His Sociocultural Milieu

Comte saw himself, and was, not only the child of his age, but also the vehicle through which his Zeitgeist found expression—through which the crucial questions of his time found a voice and a system. Comte synthesized in himself the intellectual developments and malaise of the eighteenth and early nineteenth centuries. Moreover, one of his central assumptions, which I share, was that any product of the human mind, be it a work of art, a philosophical system, or a social theory, is not created in a vacuum or in the upper reaches of its author's mind but, rather, in a concrete sociocultural matrix and intellectual climate. Such products do not come into being all at once or through one person; they unfold and mature gradually within a particular Zeitgeist in response to the existential vicissitudes of their creators.

Levy-Bruhl, in the introduction to his penetrating analysis of the work and thought of Auguste Comte, saw this clearly and enunciated a premise central not only to this book, but also to the sociology of knowledge. "Every new system of philosophy, whatever may be its apparent originality, is connected, more or less intimately, with all the doctrines which preceded it";[1] it is connected with contemporaneous social conditions, which influence it just as it may influence them. Hence he asserts that we cannot study an intellectual system without locating and interpreting it within its sociocultural context.

Levy-Bruhl, moreover, realized that this "Comtean view" could be applied to Comte's own life and intellectual system. Levy-Bruhl claims that to understand Comte's system, the historical circumstances and the general trend of contemporaneous ideas, which had an impact on Comte's life and thought, must be taken into account.[2] Levy-Bruhl, however, limited himself to showing the possibility of such a task. I will endeavor to carry out this task, not only with Comte, but with three other classical sociologists as well.

Thus, to understand Comte's—or any other social theorist's—conception of the ideal man, it will be necessary to see it in terms of his general theory of human nature. The theory of human nature will then be delineated in terms of Comte's entire intellectual system. This, in turn, will be analyzed in terms of Comte's biography and sociocultural milieu. In conclusion, the infrastructural and axiological influence of his conception of the ideal man on his intellectual system and on the course of his life will be investigated.

Auguste Comte was born at the turn of the century, in 1798, in Montpellier, France. He came into this life straddling two centuries, as he would later straddle two worlds. He sought to end the old, the ancien regime, which had led to the Revolution; and he endeavored to usher in the new, positive era. His work, therefore, like that of many persons of his time, was a social, political, philosophical, and religious answer to the problems posed by the French Revolution. Finally, Comte also picked up, and later sought to embody, the golden thread of French messianism, which had changed its language and its cultural expressions but not its central aim. Therefore, a brief discussion of the eighteenth century, the French Revolution, the nineteenth century, and the tradition of French messianism is necessary in order to understand the sociocultural milieu in which Comte lived.

The waning eighteenth century, "l'âge des lumières et de la Raison," was the age of reason and of the critical investigation by reason of all areas of human experience and speculation. It was the philosophical age par excellence, the age of intellectual ferment in which the entire sphere of knowledge was being redefined according to new values and assumptions.

The crucial problem of knowledge—of what man can know and of how he knows—was debated at length, analyzed in great detail, and cast in a new mold. The Enlightenment figures Diderot, D'Alembert, Voltaire, Condillac, La Mettrie, and others had shattered the religious and classical views of the world by rejecting the spiritual dimension of the cosmos as mere fancy and superstition. They also concentrated almost exclusively on knowledge for the purpose of obtaining power over nature so as to satisfy material and biological needs. Hence, knowledge is defined in terms of reason and observation rather than revelation. Emphasis is placed on the human being's biological organism from which consciousness is conceived of as emerging. Eighteenth-century thinkers redefined the cosmos by seeing only two great objects in it: man and the physical universe. Moreover, by emphasizing knowledge and power, it relegated love and human emotions to a secondary and inferior position. These, however, were soon to reemerge in the romantic reaction which took place during the early nineteenth century. Finally, by rejecting God and the spiritual dimension of the cosmos, the "age des lumières" also shattered the great philosophical and theological synthesis of the Middle Ages that unified and integrated human knowledge. In so doing, therefore, it had to look for a new unifying and integrating principle around which to organize and synthesize knowledge. Thus, for the rationalists and the humanists man and the psychosocial dimension became such a principle; for the scientists and empiricists the physical dimension became such a principle.

The eighteenth century, furthermore, was essentially a "critical" century, as St. Simon and Comte were to call it; it was a century of destruction—the religious, philosophical, political, and social destruction of the ancien regime which had culminated, philosophically, in the critical *Encyclopedia* of Diderot and D'Alembert and, politically, in the French Revolution. Consequently, it left to the nineteenth century, which was primarily a century of reconstruction and reaction, the erection of the new philosophical synthesis and the organization of the new sociopolitical system.

In mathematics the calculus and the theory of probability were developed, which increased the power and the prestige of the natural sciences. The social sciences began to assume their modern forms. Careful and detailed examinations of the nature and origin of the human mind and of its powers, of the development of history, and of the evolution of man were made in the light of human reason and natural law. The great success and growing prestige of physics made it the queen and model of the new sciences of man as biology was to become in the nineteenth century.

In short, every domain and discipline of human experience and speculation and all aspects of the universe were to be examined and reinterpreted by an enlightened and critical human reason, freed from the superstitions and distortions of "vested ideologies." Through critical reason and scientific observation, the natural laws of the physical universe and of man would be uncovered and man would gain power over nature and over himself. Nothing was to be considered sacred or unknowable to human intelligence, which, through the senses, was to shed light on the dark corners of human activity and on the nature of the universe.

The most significant fact of the eighteenth century is the shift from seeking to understand man and social life to attempting to change man and society. What the scientific revolution of the sixteenth and seventeenth centuries had accomplished for man's conception of nature and of the universe, the eighteenth century was now carrying out for man's conception of himself. Man becomes a physical and social being subject to the laws of nature; potentialities unfold not by God's grace but entirely by human vision and efforts. The scientific revolution, therefore, changed the view of the universe as a geocentric and living entity to that of a heliocentric and inert system. The naturalistic interpretation of man and nature now opened the way for the method of the natural sciences to be applied to the study of man and society. For, if man is essentially a natural and social being, he can be studied and analyzed by the same methods which brought such success in the natural sciences. It was hoped that a new, earthly, free, and happy life could emerge in a new, secular, free, and just society, whose foundations were anchored on the bedrock of reason.

One event towered above all others in the period during which Comte lived. This event was the French Revolution. For Comte and his contemporaries, the French Revolution was the fulcrum which related the present to the past (the eighteenth century) and the present to the future (the nineteenth century). As Comte stated:

> Without it [the French Revolution], we would have neither the theory of progress nor, therefore, a social science; and without a social science we would have no positive philosophy. Was it not necessary, therefore, that this extraordinary social event set forth, by its repercussions, a vast and prolonged movement in philosophy and political speculation? This social conflagration produced effects which differed according to the worth and originality of the minds which lived through and after it.[3]

All thinkers, great or mediocre, who grew up at the beginning of the nineteenth century, such as Turgot, Condorcet, St. Simon, Comte, Bonald, de Maistre, Bazard, Enfantin, and others, converged on one central question: what regime, or world, will be established after the Revolution, and what is our part in it? This question stimulates all the social, philosophical, and religious thought of the first half of the nineteenth century. All agreed that the fabric of French society and of the soul must be reconstructed. After the critical period, which is about to end, an organic period must follow. According to the striking expression of St. Simon: "Humanity is not made to live amidst ruins."[4]

The emerging nineteenth century, "l'age de la reconstruction et de la passion," as a reaction to the eighteenth century was a vindication of love and emotion rather than reason and cold intelligence, of passion and self-expression rather than logic and self-discipline. Above all, the nineteenth century expressed a need for reconstruction and order. Thus, speculative philosophy, seeking to unify all aspects of the universe and of human experience in overarching syntheses, reappears. As Manuel puts it: "A system in the 19th century was, by definition, an attempt to encompass all knowledge, and to dictate the rules of a new order."[5]

Politically, a reaction developed to the liberalism and the revolutionary spirit of the eighteenth century so that the political arena became divided. The progressive liberals saw in the Revolution a beginning they had to continue and to fulfill, which would, in the end, lead to the promised millennium of the new man and the new society. The romantic reactionaries, on the other hand, saw the Revolution as a great social experiment which had failed. They turned to the past, to the Middle Ages in particular, to find the secret of social order and of social integration or, in modern terms, of psychosocial unity.

To the optimistic view of human nature of the liberals, the reactionaries counterposed a pessimistic view: man is a bundle of unlimited desires and passions which must be controlled and channeled. A new integrating and unifying principle had to be found, in man or in the world, to replace the old spiritual one; a new discipline had to be found to create a psychosocial cosmos from the present chaos. Thus, it was felt that a new religion was needed that would be in harmony with the advances of human reason and science.

These are, briefly, some of the major reasons why social philosophers called the nineteenth century the "century of Reconstruction and Restoration." A reconstruction was needed that would meet the demands of a humanity entering adulthood, that is, a humanity assuming responsibility for its destiny and restoring the shattered harmony.

Auguste Comte, besides being a social thinker, a philosopher, a moralist, and a reformer, was also a prophet of the new age. As Georges Dumas writes: "Comte was a messiah, a prophet, a founder of religion and, at the same time, a philosopher and a sociologist who lived in an age which was particularly favorable to the advent of prophets and visionaries."[6] And Comte himself had once declared: "I am convinced that, before the year 1861, I will preach Positivism at Notre Dame as the only real and complete religion."[7] Comte was a prophet, but was not the only prophet of his age: La Revellière-Lepeaux, Fourier, St. Simon, Enfantin, and Bazard had also struck a messianic vein in the intellectual climate of their time.

As Michelet, Wronski, and Stark have pointed out, each nation, each culture, and each people has, deeply embedded within the fabric of its sociocultural heritage, a messianic tradition, a tradition which asserts that people and that nation to be sacred, to be God's chosen People to bring forth truth, peace, justice, and happiness for all mankind. In times when the cultural ethos and the central value system are shifting, I postulate that there are strong psychosocial forces at work to bring the messianic theme into the foreground and to give it a new cultural expression. This is precisely what happened in France at the end of the eighteenth century and during the first half of the nineteenth century. As Stark writes:

> The revolutionary age, the age in which the modern nations were born, evinced a hunger and a thirst for a new faith which can hardly be imagined more intense. Rationalistic and utilitarian ideas alone, it appears, could not satisfy the men of those days. Very deep forces were in fact stirring, and evidences of a new will to believe appeared everywhere.[8]

Sieburg, likewise, claims that the missionary ideal, the concept of a chosen people, was intensified and not weakened by the French Revolution; from the Revolution the French people acquired the notion of a national destiny and hegemony which they were chosen to carry out.[9]

This is the messianic "golden thread" to which Comte gave a social and humanistic expression in his own intellectual system; this is the great inner spiritual thrust for which he saw himself becoming the voice and, later, the representative or high priest. As Manuel concluded: "In their wildest dreams they (St. Simon, Turgot, Condorcet, Comte) never doubted for a moment that Europe was the chosen continent, France the Chosen People, and Paris the mount from which the new Gospel had to be delivered."[10]

A true heir of the eighteenth century, Comte became one of the last and, perhaps, the greatest of the encyclopedists. Like Diderot, D'Alembert, Condorcet, and St. Simon, he sought an all-inclusive synthesis of human knowledge built around a rationalist and empirical science of man and society. A true child of the Revolution, he sought, like the great minds of his generation from Bonald and de Maistre to Mme. de Staël and B. Constant, to "put an end to the Revolution" and to "close the era of anarchy and confusion" by a spiritual regeneration of human ideas and education that would lead to an enduring, or positive, social reconstruction. Comte developed one of the most comprehensive systems of thought ever devised; he explained and systematized the most recondite aspects of human nature and the minutest details of human existence. Later in his life, and well in keeping with the romantic spirit of his time, Comte experienced one of the greatest and most productive "coup de foudre" since Dante and Beatrice, which enthroned love and human emotions in the positive system thus paving the way for the religion of humanity.

In him, the two philosophical traditions of the eighteenth century, rationalism and empiricism, which had merged in science, blended with the romantic spirit. These fashioned an altogether grandiose intellectual system which claimed to reconcile and harmonize science, philosophy, and religion by reconciling order and progress, the theoretical and the practical, and man and society. These, moreover, were posited to lead eventually to a true and lasting regeneration of the human soul on the one hand, and to a reconstruction of the social system on the other.

As a man, Comte was a highly sensitive person, a keen social observer, and a brilliant intellectual who was endowed with a passionate and zealous nature, so common among the Frenchmen of the "Midi"; a nature which yearned to consecrate itself and to sacrifice its life for high and noble ideals, for a "worthy and glorious mission." Comte had a "heroic strand" well developed in him, a heroic strand which, given his time and society, could not find expression in military feats or physical prowess but only in intellectual achievements: Comte thus became a hero of thought and, later, a hero of love.

Comte's life and work had two fundamental unifying quests: that for truth and that for unity. With the first, he wanted to penetrate through the appearance of phenomena to reality, insofar as it is accessible, and to formulate a "summa of positive knowledge," which all would agree on and accept. With the second, he sought to reconcile and to synthesize the contradictory elements he found in himself and in society. The need for knowledge and security led to the most fundamental human endeavor: to know in order to improve and to perfect—first man, his physical, emotional, moral, and intellectual nature, and then the world in which he lives.

Comte formulated a theory of human cognition, a conception of the nature and origin of what we call today the sociology of knowledge. This constituted the first part, the theoretical or philosophical part of his life's work, which is embodied and elucidated in the *Cours de Philosophie Positive*. His quest for improving man and the world followed logically once he had formulated and extended a valid system of positive knowledge to all areas of human experience; it materialized and organized itself first as a positive politics and then as a positive morality: as a theory of *eudaemonia* or self-realization.

Both his theory of human cognition and his theory of eudaemonia were unified in his religion of humanity—which was to relate and to unfold all aspects of human nature and human behavior. This constituted the second, or practical, part of his life's work, which is embodied and elucidated in the *Système de Politique Positive*, in the *Catèchisme Positiviste*, and in the *Synthèse Subjective*. This he conceived as his greatest ideal, and he believed he had realized it as a sociologist-philosopher who had become the high priest of the religion of humanity.

Comte's family belonged to the "petite Bourgeoisie" of southern Provence who were described as "Catholic with fervor and Royalist with discretion."[11] Comte was most attached to his mother, from whom, so he claims, he inherited the affective and sentimental nature which Clothilde de Vaux later brought to full expression. Attending the local schools, Comte distinguished himself as both the "enfant prodige" and the "enfant terrible" of his class; moreover, he claimed that, already at a young age, he had experienced a profound need for a universal regeneration of the human spirit and of human society.[12]

While in high school, Comte met Daniel Encontre, a professor of mathematics, who, with his encyclopedic mind and his "esprit de système," greatly impressed him. Encontre was a Protestant theologian, a scientist (mathematician), and, above all, a philosopher with a deep concern for the social problems of his time. In his teachings, he sought to reconcile faith and reason, science and religion; he preached a return to order, to discipline, and to the time-proven traditions of his county. He had a profound mistrust for democratic institutions and an intense dislike for the existing social confusion. These are traits Comte was to internalize and display in his own mature thought. Comte saw Encontre as "an encyclopedic spirit, first a mathematician and a scientist but ultimately a philosopher; at ease everywhere, receptive to all the questions of his day, sensitive to the needs of his time and convinced of the necessity for order: the yet uncertain sketch of the ideal philosopher which positivism would later idealize and put forth as a leader of men."[13] Thus Encontre seems to have provided Comte with the first living model of the professor-philosopher, the ideal, "positive man." From this encounter, Comte became conscious of his vocation and life mission.

In 1814, Comte goes to Paris to continue his education at the Ecole Polytechnique where he had won a scholarship. He never graduated from that institution, which closed its doors temporarily in 1816, but he greatly benefited from the men, the ideas, and the discipline which he found there and which is later reflected in his own work. Then, in the summer of 1817, Comte met Henri de St. Simon and became his associate and collaborator and, later, even his "adopted son." This encounter proved to be one of the turning points in Comte's life and the decisive event which launched him in his "first career." Positivism will become conscious in the soul of Comte and the Zeitgeist, with the most pressing problems of the time, will reach Comte's mind through the agency of St. Simon. Georges Dumas contends that "we know the personal influence exerted by St. Simon upon Comte from 1817 to 1824. We know that during 7 years, from the age of 19 to 26, when the character is forming, Auguste Comte limited himself to receive, to organize, and to develop what he, himself, called the "idées-mères" of his master."[14] The grand aim of St. Simon, which unified his life, thoughts, and aspirations, was to put an end to the moral crisis in which humanity had been floundering since the breakdown of theological belief by formulating and organizing a new spiritual power.[15] From 1803, when he began writing, to 1825, when he died, St. Simon pursued this grand aim, which was also the object of other social thinkers of his time, with the charisma of a prophet and the zeal of a religious devotee. St. Simon, who viewed himself as the Charlemagne of philosophy and politics, wanted to replace the Catholic-feudal social system, which had finally collapsed during the Revolution, with a new scientific-industrial social system.

What finally destroyed the old theological-feudal system, for St. Simon, was the critical encyclopedia of the eighteenth century. Therefore, what would now set up the foundation for the new scientific-industrial system is the positive encyclopedia that will replace theological ideas by scientific ones in all areas of human experience. This work, the classification and completion of the positive sciences, would not be a dictionary, like the critical encyclopedia of D'Alembert and Diderot; it would be a great synthesis of all human knowledge assembled in a hierarchical scale such that one could descend from the supreme law, Newton's law of gravitation, to the minutest details of the universe, as well as ascend from the simplest empirical facts to the supreme law. This "positive" or "organic" encyclopedia would then lead, for St. Simon, to a "positive science of man" which, in turn, would put philosophy and morality on a scientific basis.

For St. Simon, as later for Comte, the chief illness of the time was that contradictory intellectual systems and explanations of the world existed side by side. The cure for this situation appeared simple enough: integrate the entire body of human knowledge into a vast positive synthesis, the positive encyclopedia, which, anchored in Newton's law of gravitation, would be the summa of modern thought.

The grand vision and aim of St. Simon was never realized by him or by any scientific or philosophical gathering of the best minds of the epoch; it was, however, "picked up" and "put onto paper," at least, by

St. Simon's young and enterprising secretary, Auguste Comte.

The essence of Comte's life and mission, the gist of his positive philosophy, the blueprint of his social reconstruction, and even the germs of his religion of humanity can be found, according to Comte himself, in his "Fundamental Pamphlet" of 1822:

> My orientation, both philosophical and social, was irrevocably set in May, 1822, by my third pamphlet in which emerged my fundamental discovery of the Sociological Law (the law of the three stages). Its very title should suffice to show the intimate relation between these viewpoints, scientific and political, which had occupied me till then but separately. . . . One cannot ignore the unity of my career, seeing thus promised, from the very beginning, the system which the present treatise alone could realize. . . . One only has to compare these pamphlets . . . to discover a constant progression, where the final aim is well defined throughout as the reorganization of the spiritual power by a renovation of philosophy.[16]

In 1823, Comte married Caroline Massin, a former prostitute with whom he had established a liaison, to prevent her arrest by the police because she had failed to report regularly to the authorities. Then, in 1826, Comte experienced a nervous breakdown which he imputed to the bad behavior of his wife and to overwork; two years later, he attempted suicide by throwing himself into the Seine from the Pont-des-Arts. In 1829, Comte, healed, reopened his course on positive philosophy, which he held at his Paris apartment. His work and insights had healed him and reinstilled enthusiasm for his great mission. Before him, he has a positive philosophy to teach and a positive polity to develop. In the center of his philosophical career, when he seeks to emulate Aristotle, Comte strives to systematize not only all human knowledge and all positive ideas, but also his own personal life, which is increasingly affected by his system. Thus he regulates his eating, sleeping, and working habits; he gives up smoking and then even drinking coffee; he develops his "cerebral diet" (that is, he ceases to read the newspapers and all current books); and finally, he will give up even women. For dessert, he will eat a piece of dry bread to remind himself of those who are hungry in the world.

With the birth of sociology, in 1838-39, as the last of the positive sciences, Comte shifts his frame of reference from the "objective method," going from the world to man, to the "subjective method," going from man to the world. Sociology becomes queen of the sciences and the means by which to evaluate and integrate all things.

Sociology, therefore, is the science that will replace theology and fulfill its basic psychosocial functions: it will study humanity and social relations rather than God and man's relation to God; and the sociologist-philosophers will become the new priesthood, the conscience and voice of humanity. The sciences, henceforth, and sociology included, do not deserve our labor if they do not contribute to improving human conditions.

In the spring of 1844, Comte meets Clothilde de Vaux and undergoes the crucial emotional transformation that will usher him into his second career, his "religious career." He will seek to become the modern St. Paul as he had sought to be the modern Aristotle in his first or "philosophical career." Comte had said: "the intellect is my guide and Lord"; now, at the beginning of his religious career to the end of his life, from the *Système* to the *Synthèse*, he will say: "love is my inspiration and my Lord." Of his meeting with Clothilde, he writes: "Religious positivism truly began with our precious meeting on May 16, 1845, when my heart spontaneously proclaimed before your stupefied family the characteristic sentence: 'one cannot always think or even work, but one can always love,' which later, when completed, became the special motto of our great work."[17]

Perhaps the most incisive description of the impact of this experience upon Comte's life and thought is the one given by Boris Sokoloff:

> The human elements which were denied to Comte before now came with Clothilde as an inrushing flood. Now he was ready to accept love as an initiation to philosophy. Love and human emotions are henceforth seen as indispensable elements for positive philosophy. It was through Clothilde, who became the model of perfection and the ideal woman, that the deeper truths of human existence were revealed to him. Through her, he purified his soul and found the missing element in his philosophical system: he transformed the philosophy of pure intellect into a system based on emotions, on human feeling, on love. From being under the pre-eminence of the "esprit de géometrie" he now passed to the "esprit de finesse."[18]

In the *Cours* Comte had substituted humanity for God and science for religion; now the program of the *Système* is to reorganize society without God or kings. As the *Cours* had systematized all thoughts, so now the *Système* is to systematize all human emotions. This systematization of all psychic and social activity, of the inner life as well as the social life of man, which turned out to be Comte's underlying lifelong objective, was to be completed by a systematization of all human behavior in his last great work, the *Synthèse Subjective*, which was begun in 1856 but never finished.

Clothilde, who died on 5 April 1846, provided Comte with the link, which he had sought in vain in philosophy, to connect him with humanity at an existential level, as she had provided the link to connect the "head" with the "heart" in his intellectual system. As Gouhier, Comte's biographer, writes:

> Human activity is a communion, to love is to feel this unity and to participate joyfully in this communion . . . Auguste Comte never loved Humanity better than in loving Clothilde, therefore, one must love humanity as Comte loved Clothilde. His fundamental experience has a universal value: it represents the perfect model of the gift which all men must give Humanity. The love of Comte for Clothilde has spontaneously become adoration, silent prayer, and daily cult: the love of man for Humanity.[19]

In 1848 Comte published a "discours sur l'Ensemble du Positivisme" and proclaimed himself high priest of humanity. In that year, he also founded the Société Positiviste, which was to be the nucleus of the new spiritual power which would reorganize French and European society.

At the end of his life, Comte saw, in his dreams, his religion of humanity penetrating into and regenerating the world; he saw himself preaching positivism from Notre Dame and he wrote letters to Louis XVIII, to the czar, to the General of the Jesuits, and to French senators and Turkish pashas to enlighten them and to entreat them to join forces with him. On 5 September 1857, after having cast a last glance on the relics of his "Sainte Clothilde," Auguste Comte died peacefully in his apartment at 5, Rue Monsieur le Prince, in Paris. Thus his science of humanity developed and organized through positive philosophy, reached its apex and fulfillment in sociology and finally transformed itself and culminated, through his experiences and love for Clothilde, into the religion of humanity.

Comte's Theory of Human Nature and His Conception of the Ideal Man

Most classical social thinkers have sought to have an influence not only upon social thought but also upon social evolution, that is, to connect thought and action, vision and realization, and science and politics. They have, therefore, included both the descriptive and the normative aspects, value facts and value judgments into their theories, and none has systematized this dialectical relationship more thoroughly and felt it more passionately than Auguste Comte. Comte was not only a classical social thinker and a great sociologist; he was also a great humanist and a philosopher in the deepest sense; he saw human nature as the axis of creation and he sought to understand man in his totality and to actualize that which is highest in human nature.

Thus, there is perhaps no better writer than Auguste Comte with whom to begin a study of the "conception of ideal man in classical sociology"; for he had, relatively speaking, a clear and explicit theory of human nature and well articulated notions as to what the "ideal man," the man of the future whom he saw himself as representing, would be like and should be like.

For Comte, the project of human life should be "to know in order to improve and to perfect" first humanity, and then the world—which, for him, are the two fundamental objects of all human studies. Thus, in the *Cours* he explicitly declared: "the study of man and of the external world necessarily constitutes the double and eternal subject of all our philosophical conceptions."[20] Later, in his *Système,* he added: "When theology proclaimed its fundamental precept 'to know in order to improve,' it only formulated the spontaneous tendencies of the universal instinct."[21] This is what positivism will now fully systematize and develop on a durable philosophical foundation. Underlying "to know man and the external world" stands a theory of human cognition on which "a solid philosophical foundation" for a science of man can be developed; underpinning "to improve and to perfect man and the world" stands a theory of eudaemonia, a pathway to self-realization by which to expand human consciousness and to actualize man's higher potentialities and faculties; and this theory of eudaemonia itself, I contend, rests upon a conception of the ideal man, Comte's vision of the good man leading the good life in the good society.

Comte states that the essence of progress consists "essentially, for the individual as for the species, in making prevail more and more the eminent attributes which distinguish our humanity from our animality, that is, our intelligence and sociability, faculties which are naturally related";[22] it consists in rendering man more human. Human action ensures the unfoldment of the scientific spirit and the ultimate triumph of positivism, but positivism is the consequence and not the cause of the development of the human spirit, that is, of human intelligence. For Comte, action on nature develops along with intelligence, while intelligence articulates and constructs the tools—the natural sciences—for bringing this about. Thus civilization consists, on the one hand, in the development of the human spirit and, on the other, in the action of man on nature. For him, it is the "state of civilization," therefore, which determines the form of social organization and which provides the central value system of society.[23]

Comte's first aim in life was to be a social reformer and to reconstruct European society, which he saw as permeated by anarchy, disorder, and strife. His second aim was to be a scientist and a philosopher. These goals were the driving forces and the integrating principles during that period when he saw intelligence as the supreme force organizing and directing social action. Later science and philosophy became only the necessary preamble to the development of a religion of humanity, which alone, by its systematic unfoldment of the capacity to love, could realize the social reform, the psychosocial unity, which he had postulated as the grand aim of his life.

After the initiation of love, the science of man becomes the religion of humanity, and Comte, the scientist, the philosopher, and the social engineer, becomes Comte the prophet, the high priest of humanity, and the moralist. Social integration depends on a transformation of the human heart and an unfoldment and realization of human consciousness. Since the whole of human history leads to the realization of that which is highest in human nature and of the fundamental order of society;[24] since man and civilization are now entering the "positive age," the age of maturity, it is the religion of humanity which will give unity to Comte's aims and strivings, which will turn his intellectual edifice into a true system, and which will make possible the realization of that fundamental psychosocial unity which was always Comte's grand objective.

The relationship between Comte's theory of human nature, his theory of the nature of society, his theory of the nature of history, and his conception of sociology is clear: his theory of the nature of society represents, essentially, the structural or static aspects of the expression and unfoldment of human nature; his theory of the nature of history represents the dynamic or functional aspects of the expression and unfoldment of human nature—its becoming. For, in the final analysis, society, history, and civilization are seen by Comte as nothing other than the expression and realization of the potentialities of human nature and the great mirror, or social laboratory, in which we may see them in action and study them positively. This is one of the basic reasons why he elaborated such an intricate and precise set of homologies between man's psyche and society, between the human microcosm and the social macrocosm, which is but an externalization and crystallization of the former. His conception of the nature of his discipline, the positive system which grows and unfolds from science to religion through philosophy, is, likewise, but the expression of the means by which man may know and improve himself, as well as the world in which he lives. It is the articulation of a theory of human cognition and its systematic application to the study of man and society.

Comte's conception of the ideal man can be found in and abstracted from both his personal life and his intellectual system. To be properly understood, however, it must be related to and explained within the perspective of his theory of human nature, of which it is the highest development.

The theory of human nature is composed of three major parts: *the objective part*, his *Tableau Cérébrale; the subjective part*, the study of civilization through the law of the three stages; and *the normative part*, his conception of the ideal man.

The Objective Part. Comte first developed his *Tableau Cérébrale* around 1836-37 while he was developing his hierarchy of the sciences. He formulated it while abstracting and generalizing the basic methods and results of biology in the works of Bichat and Gall. It is Gall's phrenological theories which later became, when Comte refined them, his *Tableau Cérébrale*. Comte stated that the *Tableau Cérébrale* "summarizes all that which has been truly demonstrated in the positive theory of human nature"[25] and that the best use of the cerebral scheme consisted in formulating the fundamental problem of human life: the ascendency of sociability over personality or that of altruism over egoism.[26]

The objective aspect of Comte's theory of human nature, however, had to be completed by the subjective method developed by sociology and by its functional aspects as revealed by social and historical studies. Thus Comte writes: "It is of sociology that biology must ask the true theory of the highest functions of humanity. . . . Biology can only develop worthily this grand subject by subordinating itself to sociology which alone is truly competent [to deal with it]."[27]

According to this scheme, human nature, the essence of which can be found in the brain, is subdivided into three fundamental systems: the heart *(le coeur)*, which provides the energy and drive for the human personality; the intelligence *(l'esprit)*, which counsels and steers the human personality; and the character *(le caractère)*, which acts and executes, through human behavior, the drives of the first and the ideas of the second. Comte, therefore, sees three fundamental systems as operative in man: the affective, the speculative, and the active, by which man feels, thinks, and acts. Interestingly enough, Comte identified the will with the emotions, seeing it as "constituting only the last state of desire (affection), when mental deliberation has recognized the convenience of an impulse."[28]

The ideal structural relations among these three fundamental components of human nature, Comte presents in an aphoristic fashion "to act by affection and to think in order to act."[29] In simpler words, Comte's *Tableau Cérébrale* presents human nature as being made up of and expressing itself through three basic systems: the driving force, the guiding light, and the executive structure. The theory can be illustrated by picturing a man in a horse carriage. The man who steers the carriage represents the intelligence, the horse that draws it represents the affections, and the carriage which executes and realizes the foregoing represents his actions.

During his first career, Comte focused his investigations essentially on the intelligence, for then "reason was his Lord"; but, in his second career, after his great love experience, love becomes his lord, and then the affections become the cornerstone of his system.

At first, Comte thought that intelligence was the fundamental faculty and determinant of action; later, he came to the conclusion that both intelligence and activity are but means to an end and that the end, an end in itself, was love. Thus the "insurrection of the spirit against the heart" must cease; science and religion must not fight each other any more as they have in the last centuries; they must complement each other so that science and knowledge will be the handmaidens of religion and love, which, together, will bring about the much desired and needed psychosocial unity. Comte's grand aim, therefore, is a perfect coordination between the three systems of human nature, with each performing its natural function to the fullest extent possible. He hoped to realize this aim through his religion of humanity.

Each of the three systems of human nature corresponds to, and is stimulated by, a certain area of the brain. Moreover, each system is further subdivided and assigned a given relationship with the external world. Thus the intelligence is correlated with the anterior part of the brain because for Comte thinking is located near the organs of perception; the heart is correlated to the posterior part of the brain because the emotions are directly related to the locomotive centers; and character is in the middle of the brain between thinking and feeling, which both affect it and feed it.

The heart is subdivided into egoism, the personal inclinations or "instincts," and altruism, the social inclinations or "instincts." Egoism, or personality, is subdivided into seven instincts or motors. The three instincts of conservation are the nutritive, the sexual, and the maternal. The two instincts of improvement are the destructive or military and the constructive or industrial. And the two instincts of ambition are the need for approbation (psychological), pride, and the need for domination (material), vanity. Altruism, or sociability is subdivided into three key instincts or motors: attachment, veneration, and goodness, or universal sympathy.

The intelligence, or speculative nature, is subdivided into conception and expression. Conception can be either active or passive. Passive conception, or contemplation, can be analytic or synthetic. Active conception, or meditation, can be inductive or deductive.

> There are two types of conceptions: one passive, the other active. In man, the first is called Contemplation, the second Meditation. By the first, the intelligence receives the primitive materials of all its constructions from the outside—ideas! While Meditation produces those constructions—thoughts.[30]

Finally, the character, or active nature, is courageous, prudent, and persevering.

> The three practical virtues are, by themselves, indifferent to good and evil, they are directed only to action. As for the five intellectual functions, their true aim consists evidently in serving the three social inclinations rather than the seven personal inclinations. This is the only way for their influence to become important and durable.[31]

This cerebral scheme and its systematic development enabled Comte to talk about the fundamental problem of social life, the transformation and purification of the human heart. "This cerebral scheme illuminates the great human problem of the subordination of Egoism to Altruism. The question is such that the three social instincts assisted by the five intellectual functions overcome the habitual impulse of the seven personal inclinations, reducing these to their indispensible satisfactions, to consecrate the three active organs to the service of sociability."[32] Later, he added that "if the intellect does not betray its holy mission,"[33] the personality, which is by its very nature undisciplined, will become subordinated to sociability and serve its ends. Then harmony will be established between affection, intelligence, and activity and this will enable man to express his true nature.

This physiological organization, in which function and interrelation determine location, explains why positivism undertook the task of systematizing consecutively human thinking, then human actions, and finally human feelings. "Positivism has three necessary preparations relative first to intelligence, then to activity, and finally to affectivity. To these correspond the Greek elaboration, the Roman incorporation, and the Catholic-feudal initiations."[34]

This organization also has other implications, chief of which is that while the intelligence and the character are at rest, the heart continues its activity unceasingly, which makes it the center of both unity and continuity in the human personality and in the social system.

Finally, Comte associated his *Tableau Cérébrale* with the following postulates. One pertains to the heart and the other to the intelligence.

"There is a decrease of energy (strength) and an increase of 'dignity' and 'nobility' going from the back forward, from below upwards, and from the borders to the center."[35] This particular Comteian conception is such that the nutritive instinct, followed by the sexual instinct, has the greatest natural strength and the least "dignity" and "nobility"; but goodness, followed by veneration, has the least energy and the greatest "dignity" and "nobility." The central problem of the human heart is also the central problem of society: how to subordinate egoism, which is naturally stronger, to altruism, which is naturally weaker or, as Comte would say, how to make sociability prevail over personality. This means that, when man is left by himself—man in nature—he will not be able to achieve this basic transformation. For this task he needs a social discipline and a moral art, which Comte hopes positivism will provide.

"To see in order to know, to know in order to foresee or predict, and to predict in order to ameliorate," is summarized as "savoir pour prevoir afin de pourvoir."[36] This is the central program of the intelligence as expressed in the *Cours:* all positive knowledge derives from observation. (Later Comte added that positive knowledge derived from personal experience as well.) Positive knowledge, gathered from the world and from society, enables prediction according to "natural laws." Prediction is important for improving both social conditions and human nature.

The first postulate beautifully summarizes the central problem and quest of Comte's second career as the second postulate encapsulates the central problem and aim of his first career. This, however, is as far as the objective method will take us in anchoring the positive theory of human nature in biology or in "phrenological physiology."[37] He turns to the subjective method outlined in his sociology to complete his theory of human nature.

The Subjective Part. The first fundamental point that Comte makes from the subjective perspective of sociology is that human nature should be looked for and analyzed, in its higher manifestations, not in the individual but in the species, in humanity. Humanity, which Comte termed the "great being," is analyzed as it unfolds through history and manifests itself in successive civilizations. Here the static and the dynamic aspects of the subjective approach are to be found in the biography of the great being (the history of human societies) and in the stages of its products (human civilizations). In hypostatizing his great being, Comte drew on Pascal's conception of the universal man[38] and utilized the analogy of the "body social" on a grand scale, though with certain reservations and qualifications. Not all people are to be incorporated in the great being, only the worthy ones. Comte, moreover, admitted fundamental differences between the "body social" and the "body physical."

The *Tableau Cérébrale* and its components are projected into the social system and homologized into various groups and dynamics. The cerebral scheme becomes a giant map of human society providing us with the static components and their interrelations in the social system just as the law of the three stages, its dynamic complement, will reveal to us the pattern of their unfoldment, differentiation, and realization. The *Tableau Cérébrale*, therefore, becomes also the foundation and the blueprint for the religion of humanity. The human brain, with its localized functions and expressions of the human soul, is now externalized and reified in the life and expressions of the great being.

Accordingly, Comte distinguishes among three basic "social tissues" or classes: the women correspond to the heart and activate love, feeling, and morality; the priesthood corresponds to intelligence and activates thinking, reason, and knowledge, which are now the servants of the heart; and the patriciate, striving for order, and the proletariat, emphasizing progress, correspond to and carry out social activity.

The static foundations of the religion of humanity are similarly derived from the cerebral scheme. Its three divisions are correlated with and correspond to the three systems of human nature. Thus the positive cult corresponds to the heart and is devised to systematize all human affections, to unfold and realize the higher ones (the social ones) and to inhibit and suppress the lower ones (the personal ones). The positive dogma corresponds to the intelligence and is devised to systematize all thoughts according to the hierarchy of the sciences, and to unfold human intelligence to its fullest. Finally, the *positive Regime* corresponds to activity and is devised to systematize all human actions along the most constructive and productive lines.

The positive theory of education is, in like manner, established upon the cerebral scheme and has a threefold subdivision. The first deals with effective development and takes place in the family, under the supervision of women, of the mother in particular. The second deals with the speculative or theoretical development and takes place in the church, in the positive temple, under the supervision of the sociologist-philosopher turned "positive Priest of Humanity." Finally, the third deals with the active, or practical development, and takes place in the city *(la Cité)*, that is, in society, under the supervision and rule of the patriciate, the bankers and industrialists.

Comte, with his obsession for systematic and analogical typologies, related all the great social, psychological, and philosophical problems of his time to his *Tableau Cérébrale* and he interpreted them in strict accordance with his theory of human nature. Thus the fundamental problem of human life, the great quest for unity, with its threefold subordination of the problem of the intellect, or knowledge, of the problem of the heart, or of morality, and of the problem of the character, or of activity, is rooted in his cerebral scheme together with its solution. The solution is to establish harmony between intellect, heart, and character so as to achieve the fullest natural development and expression of each in social life. Accordingly, Comte tells us: "If the solution of the human problem begins in childhood, individually or collectively, in subordinating Egoism to Altruism, it continues during adolescence by the theoretical subordination of analysis to synthesis; and then the active life comes to complete and consolidate it in subordinating irrevocably progress to order."[39]

Thus, the problem of human knowledge, the subordination of imagination to observation, is to give predominance to contemplation over meditation so that all subjective constructions of the spirit can be grounded in the outer, objective, world through empirical data. The subordination of analysis to synthesis, likewise, implies that, within contemplation, we should adopt the sociological rather than the cosmological viewpoint. Observations should be related to humanity rather than to the world—all specific knowledge should always be related to the whole, that is, to humanity, in view of utility and not for the sake of knowledge per se. All knowledge and activity have one fundamental aim: the satisfaction of basic needs and wants and, later, the unfoldment of love.

The problem of love or morality, the subordination of egoism to altruism similarly consists in stressing and developing the three social instincts (veneration, attachment, and goodness) while inhibiting and controlling the three personal instincts (the nutritive, sexual, and maternal). Comte, seeing himself as the prototype of the man of the future, sought to realize this ideal by leading an ascetic life—giving up tobacco, wine, coffee, and sex, and by helping others as much as he could. For Comte, the solution to this problem begins in the family, which provides the most fundamental and elementary form of social life.

The unfoldment of social feelings begins in the family. Filial affection gives rise to veneration for our parents and elicits a feeling of continuity which links man with humanity's past. Then fraternal affection awakens the feeling of solidarity and links man with the present. Finally moral education is completed by conjugal and by paternal feelings, which teach man how to care for his successors and which link him with the future.[40]

The problem of activity, the subordination of progress to order, is somewhat more complex than it would appear at first sight. It is not simply the instincts of conservation versus those of improvement. For Comte, order is essentially the opposite of anarchy, which he saw as the "major illness" of his age. Anarchy is not only the lack of harmony between the systems of human nature, but also a lack of harmony between the various classes and forces operating in society, which are externalizations of human nature. Order, therefore, is the proper harmony and relationship between the intelligence, the heart, and activity and between the corresponding classes in society, whereby each fulfills its "natural" function to the fullest extent possible. Progress, on the other hand, is the development of each of these along its spontaneous line of evolution; it is the realization and actualization of that which is distinctively human, and of the various social functions. By subordinating progress to order, Comte means that harmony between the various parts of human nature and of society, upon which unity depends, is paramount and that the growth and development of each of these aspects should be harmonious and gradual and never threaten the underlying unity by growth of one level at the expense of another.

For Comte, Greek civilization concentrated on intellectual growth, Roman civilization focused on the unfoldment of activity, and the Catholic-feudal system of the Middle Ages gave affective development the predominant place. This uneven development led to the Renaissance and the Reformation ending up in the Enlightenment, which produced the "insurrection of the intelligence against the heart" with its dreadful consequences—moral and social chaos. Positive philosophy, sociology, and the religion of humanity will now set about to harmonize the unfoldment and interrelationship of the head, the heart, and the character, both individually and collectively, in man and in society, and establish the true psychosocial unity which is the highest goal of human history.

Comte's law of the three stages, which gave him fundamental insights into human and social evolution, is rooted in his theory of human nature. The law of the three stages is the progressive evolution of intelligence, activity, and affections in man, in society, and in the great being. Thus the human "spirit" passes through three basic stages: the theological, the metaphysical, and the positive. These stages correspond to the three basic types of knowledge and conceptions of the world: the fictitious or imaginary, the abstract or ontological, and the positive or experiential. To the three stages of the human intelligence are correlated the three fundamental stages of development of human activity: conquest, defense, and production. In his second career, Comte also added to these the three stages of the unfoldment of the heart: the domestic, the civic, and the universal, or the love of family, nation, and humanity.

Intimately related to his law of the three stages is Comte's "classification of the sciences" or "encyclopedic hierarchy," which is its "indispensable complement." It is the theoretical framework, validated by history, in which we can trace the progressive unfoldment of the human spirit. This classification, which is both logical and empirical, shows the gradual development of mathematics, astronomy, physics, chemistry, biology, sociology, and morality. The internal divisions of each science pass through each of the three stages and become increasingly complex, concrete, and practical. One of the chief implications of this "encyclopedic hierarchy" is the assertion that as phenomena increase in complexity and concreteness, they become more modifiable; more laws and processes deal with them and this allows for greater "choice of emphasis." Physical phenomena are at the bottom of the hierarchy and social and moral phenomena at the top; this means that the latter are most amenable to improvement and perfection.

As there is a hierarchy of the sciences, so there must be a hierarchy of scientists; sociologist-philosophers, the priests of humanity, are at the top, and mathematicians (the geometricians against whom Comte felt particularly bitter) are at the bottom. The hierarchy of scientists has its correlate in the sphere of activity where their agents are likewise classified according to the degree of complexity, importance, and usefulness of their functions.

Bankers and industrialists are at the top of the hierarchy and, therefore, constitute the government, which must always remain, however, subordinated to the spiritual power. For the affective sphere, Comte did not unfold a full "hierarchy of love" with its ministers, but he did develop an embryonic classification. He stated that three basic social instincts are activated and developed by three "guardian angels": the mother who elicits and unfolds veneration in her child connects it with the past; the wife or sweetheart who elicits and unfolds attachment is a connection with the present; and the daughter who elicits and unfolds goodness or universal love is a connection with the future.

Why is Comte so concerned with establishing hierarchies, with setting up isomorphic correspondences, and with systematizing and categorizing the entire human universe? Because he had a deep need for unity, for harmony, in which every single aspect of the known universe must be related to the whole of humanity and find its proper place in the world. "True philosophy proposes to systematize, as much as possible, *the whole of human existence*, individual and collective, considered in the three orders of phenomena which characterize it—thoughts, feelings, and actions."[41]

The hierarchies, the correspondences, and the systematizations extend the "great chain of Being," preserve harmony, and insure unity. Underlying the foregoing set of correspondences and homologies between the human brain, the psyche, and human society, and their correlated unfoldment through history, stand two fundamental themes.

First, all human faculties and powers, whether physiological, psychological, or social, are developed by exercise and repetition and are inhibited and atrophied by inactivity and nonuse. Therefore, to unfold a faculty or power, one must use it as much as possible; but to decrease and inhibit a faculty or power, one need only to not use it. This is one of the reasons why positive morality always stresses "dynamic morality," as Bergson called it, over "static morality"; it means doing what is good rather than seeking desperately to control what is negative. This is also what, so Comte claims, distinguishes positive morality from the theological religions it replaced; positivism emphasizes doing good and Christianity focuses on controlling and curbing evil.

Second, human faculties and powers are awakened and developed through human interaction; people bring out and elicit potentialities and traits which we, ourselves, did not even suspect we possessed; human interaction is the catalyst by which potentialities are translated into actualities, by which the distinctively human traits, intelligence and love, are awakened and developed. To "live for others" is, in fact, to live for oneself or, rather, for the best that is in oneself, for the great being. Every action in the world has an immediate reaction in us, activating and developing certain faculties and traits in our nature while inhibiting others. To live for others is to realize to the fullest our own nature, faculties, and potentialities.

Man's entire social life, the whole framework of society and history is, for Comte, a great school, and the fundamental aim of life is education. Education humanizes; it socializes and stimulates the capacity to love and know. The history of human societies is thus the history of human education and self-realization, which is at first spontaneous, or unconscious, and then systematic, or conscious. And the great being is the product of such an education.

To conclude then, Comte is a positivist and not an existentialist or a transcendentalist. In the world as we know it —and what we know is but a fraction of the reality that is forever beyond our grasp—there is no absolute creation; all is a progressive unfoldment of potentialities which are preexistent in the species. Science is the systematic development of natural and spontaneous common sense; religion is the systematic development of the natural religious instincts (the need for harmony and unity); and universal love or goodness is the fullest expression of intrinsic "altruistic instincts." Human nature and human civilization are the progressive unfoldment and expression of latent potentialities intrinsic to human nature.

The evolution and unfoldment of human nature and consciousness is first spontaneous, then it is systematic. In Comte's language, this means that evolution is at first unconscious, instinctive, and blind, and then, with maturity and experience, it becomes conscious, deliberate, and rationally directed. For humanity to enter the positive stage, the age of maturity, means that what was first unconscious will now become conscious; human consciousness will now permeate human existence and human experience. It also means that the center of gravity of psychosocial life will shift from fiction and abstractions, and from the world, to humanity. As Comte himself declared: "Evolution is nothing but the realization of human nature."[42] Hence, to know human nature, we must study it objectively and subjectively, statically and dynamically, not in the individual but in the great being, in humanity, through history which is the biography of human becoming.

Throughout his life Comte was in search of a system which would enable man to establish a psychosocial harmony. This need for unity led Comte to religion. Positive philosophy is his first religion, the scientific religion of the head; the religion of humanity is his second religion, the religion of the heart—and both take sociology as their axis. Religion, moreover, always remains that which binds and unites, that which produces harmony.

During his first career, Comte saw the fundamental object of religion as that of binding and uniting the "spirits" of men, that is, their minds, with a common value system and conception of the universe. During his second career, he saw an even more important function for it: to bind men's "hearts" and emotions for this would generate a true psychosynthesis and social integration. During his first career, Comte believed that only a synthesis of all positive knowledge could create a social and psychological unity; but, in his second career, he realized that only love would produce the fundamental unity he sought all his life.

The great being needs the achievements of its members; the great being subsists and unfolds only if, in each generation, it finds servants who work to "receive, increase, and transmit" to future generations that which they have received. This is why the great being is a hypostatization of "worthy men of good will," of the highest and noblest in human nature, and why egoism is no more a part of it than the parasite is a part of the organism on which it lives. The help which the individual finds in humanity is immense for it represents that which accumulated and grew since the dawn of time. And it is this which accounts for the fact that Comte saw in the great being man's triple positive providence—the affective, intellectual, and material.

The new spiritual power Comte sought to institute and to head will not use material means of coercion such as force, threats, economic reprisals, or imprisonment; it will use only reason, sympathy, and persuasion by living example; all other means would be contrary to human dignity. Comte stressed obedience, but only a voluntary obedience, which is the free adhesion to a demonstrated faith rather than blind obedience to authority or revelation. Thus Comte stressed education and he structured his intellectual system so that it would be a giant organic system of education. The temporal power, however, will use means of social control because it must use them. "Conscience and education would often be powerless against daily infractions, if the temporal power did not apply physical repressions."[43] But the temporal power must always be subjected to the spiritual power which uses only "means of socialization." Although Comte recognized the need for both socialization and social controls, he clearly placed greater emphasis on education.

For Comte, therefore, man as a biological organism is a natural phenomenon; but man as a member of humanity is a social and religious phenomenon. The biological organism, the brain in particular, contains all human potentialities, but it is only through society, through the great being, that these potentialities can be realized. In consequence, Comte sees human beings neither as completely egoistical and selfish, nor as naturally good and altruistic but, rather, as having potentialities for both altruism and egoism. These possibilities exist in all people, but must be actualized.

This is why "to live for others" became the categorical imperative of positivism and why Comte saw human nature as sociocentric. For

Comte, a person who loves no one, who lives only for himself without a "social life" remains a person *in posse*. It is society, a regulated network of social relations, which leads from animality to humanity. "Any man or animal who loves nothing and who lives only for himself finds himself thereby condemned to an unhappy oscillation between an ignoble torpor and a disorderly agitation. To live for others thus becomes the summary of the whole of positive morality."[44]

Moreover, as the coarser tendencies and instincts are naturally more powerful and vital than the nobler and more refined ones, a man left by himself, without a social discipline and a personal morality, would remain egoistical and selfish, a brute or an animal. But by conscious effort and a properly organized set of social relations instituted by positive morality, man will be able to realize and to actualize his finer potentialities and his nobler possibilities; he will be able to humanize himself and to develop his distinctively human faculties: love, knowledge, and morality.

The Normative Part. Comte's theory of human nature contains a conception of the ideal man, not just what man is, structurally and functionally. The theory explains not only how man became what he is, but also what he will and should become. This conception of the ideal man, together with the theory of human nature, stands, as I have already shown, preconsciously as well as consciously, infrastructurally, and axiologically, behind his cognitive system, giving it an orientation, a goal to strive for, and a raison d'être.

Specifically, how did this conception emerge and unfold throughout his life and, finally, how did it affect his work? These are questions I shall now explore further. During his first career, Comte sees persons essentially as thinking and acting beings; thoughts and ideas, through emotions and feelings, structure and guide behavior. If thought is unified then emotions and behavior will be unified. This, in turn, will unify society. A positive synthesis of human knowledge will, therefore, accomplish what religion formerly achieved: a communion of minds and actions. Thoughts, moreover, are essentially aimed at controlling nature in order to satisfy basic needs. This implies that the harnessing of nature will provide both the test and the stimulus for man's thought system—and once it can be shown that reason's ideas are related to and can affect physical objects, the triumph of science and positivism will be ensured.

During his second career, however, Comte shifted his emphasis. He discovered and experienced the power of love so that now love takes the ascendancy in his thought and positive system. He comes to see man more as a feeling and thinking being and less as a thinking and acting being. Positive religion will be more than a synthesis of positive knowledge uniting minds; it will be a theoretical and practical doctrine uniting hearts and feelings and, through these, human nature and society will be united.

In the distant future, moreover, when people are exonerated from physical activity to satisfy basic material needs, "pure consciousness," the distinctively human characteristic will unfold to an unparalleled extent in the history of mankind. At that time intelligence will truly serve the three social instincts of the heart, rather than activity and industry. Then cold scientific theories and rational industrial schemes will be superseded by esthetic expressions, social activities, and games and feasts to an extent not yet dreamed of.

The "ideal man" is the man of the future, the mature man; the man of the past was the immature child. But the man of the present is the adolescent of the "Sturm und Drang," a young man caught in an anarchic hiatus between two psychosocial cosmoses and two ages. The ideal man is now the positive man, that is, the sociocentric lover, knower, and servant of humanity, as he was always the man who, in his age, is as far advanced, in evolutionary terms, as he can be. Thus, for instance, in the age of fetishism the ideal man stood for polytheism; in the age of polytheism, he stood for monotheism; and in the age of monotheism, he stood for the metaphysical world view. The ideal man is what Hegel called the "welthistorische Persönlichkeit"—the man whose personality is part of the vanguard of history.

The ideal man is he who lives for others, consciously and systematically subordinating personal thoughts, sentiments, and actions to humanity. He consciously and deliberately realizes higher social instincts and inclinations while, at the same time, inhibiting and suppressing lower instincts and inclinations. He knows what society and history are and consciously works to bring about their fullest unfoldment and realization.

The ideal man, for Comte, is the man who has humanized himself by developing his capacity to know, to love, and to work constructively for the common good. He is the man who can truly say "nihil humanum a me alienum puto"; he is open to all human experiences and can relate meaningfully and creatively with everyone, having actualized as much as possible of his human nature. He is fully conscious, fully altruistic and, therefore, fully alive.

The ideal man has renounced seeking and studying that which he cannot know, that which is secondary, vain, and useless. He seeks what is primary, beneficial, and useful for all mankind. He knows humanity in order to improve it and, through humanity, he knows and improves himself. Comte's ideal man accepts the fact that he cannot reach and possess absolutes; all he can ever reach is relative; he knows both his limits and his potentialities. He is aware of his infinite debt to humanity and of his necessary subordination to the great being; he strives for order through progress and for progress through order. He cultivates the love of others and by his example (actions), his being (love), and his words and writings (knowledge), seeks to bring others to do likewise. Finally and especially, the ideal man, the positive man, is the man who has reached a unity and a harmony with humanity and, through humanity, with himself, and with the world. He has identified with, and committed himself to, the development and expression of that which is highest, noblest, and most human in humanity and, therefore, in himself.

In Comte's words: "Having become more synthetic, more synergic, and more sympathetic, human nature tends towards the systematic unfoldment of that which is highest in it by the rising preponderance of altruism over egoism."[45] And, as he explains further: "Universal education makes us first more sympathetic and then more synthetic, only to prepare us to be more synergic. . . . Sympathy is the union of hearts; synthesis, the intellectual order, is the harmony of the spirit within itself and with others; synergy is the convergence of these in activity."[46]

At first, Comte thought that synergy presupposed only synthesis, but later he realized that synthesis itself presupposed sympathy. The ideal man embodies and realizes the maxim of the *Imitatio Christi:* "To love Thee above all and to love myself only because of Thee," but he substitutes humanity for Christ.

Comte's conception of the ideal man is outlined in his conception of God—humanity or the great being. The concept of God contains conceptions of the highest good and the ultimate model for men to emulate. The dream of deification, the vision of becoming like God is endemic to the history of human thought and of human civilization. The concept of God includes man's chief ideal of what he could strive for and become. One of the fundamental axioms of the Eastern Christian church indicates this very clearly when it states: "God has become man, so that man may become God."

Comte accepted the basic assumption that one of the fundamental functions of the concept of God is to serve as man's supreme ideal and model. Thus he identified the history of religion with the biography of the unfoldment of human intelligence; and he declared that the various transcendental Gods were dramatized projections of human wishes, desires, aspirations, fears, and ideals. He claimed that theological religion, in subordinating man to a fiction whose center of gravity lay outside of man and his real needs, would retard improvement and self-realization during adulthood. Positive religion, on the other hand, would accelerate the unfoldment and realization of human nature precisely because it is conscious.

The concept of God always embodied the substance of the highest ideals of man: that supreme ideal of truth, reality, love, goodness, and life which he sought to unite with and to incarnate at various stages of his evolution. Comte's conception of God, expressed in the cultural terms proper to his age and society, is no different; it symbolizes and synthesizes his view of the ideal man, the supreme ideal which he sought to embody and to preach to others. If men in past epochs projected their ideals onto their Gods, Comte does precisely the same, projecting the unspoken and half-conscious wishes and ideals of the Zeitgeist in which he lived.

A cursory analysis of four of Comte's basic statements about the great being will readily confirm these insights.

"Humanity is the whole [*ensemble*] of past, future, and present beings. The term 'whole' indicates here . . . not all men but only those who are truly worthy by their true cooperation."[47] Thus all people are called to become part of humanity. All have the potentialities to do so, but only the worthy ones, who have striven to unfold and actualize their highest potentialities, are actually incorporated in the great being.

"Around the great being, the immediate motor of each existence, individual or collective, our affections concentrate as spontaneously as do all our thoughts and actions."[48] The great being is the unifying and integrating principle for thoughts, feelings, and actions, and represents Comte's supreme ideal for man. Moreover, the great being can be realized only by the conscious and free choice of "independent wills" and can be "dissolved" by actions falling short of the ideal.

"We do not adore [humanity] as the old God to compliment her but to serve her better in improving ourselves."[49] Worship of the great being has the direct and explicit aim of improving and perfecting man in order to improve humanity, in contradistinction to that of the theological gods where this aim, though still there, was indirect and implicit.

"[We] conceive therefore the Great Being as being such as we are but to a more pronounced degree, driven by feeling, enlightened by intelligence, and sustained by activity."[50] The great being represents an idealized conception of man but with the same fundamental attributes highlighted and further actualized.

Taken together, these four basic statements characterize Comte's great being as a projection, externalization, and crystallization of his conception of the ideal man, or the essence of humanity, which each person should strive to actualize.

The Ideal Man in Comte's Life and Intellectual System

Already in his youth, Comte was seeking a conception of an ideal man to develop and to become. In his adulthood, he claimed he had found it, and in his mature years, he sought to live and incarnate it.

His encounter and brief relation with Daniel Encontre at the Lycée of Montpellier gave him the first glimpse of this ideal man. Encontre was the true philosopher with an "esprit de synthèse," the true professor seeking to reconcile religion, philosophy, science, with one another, and order with progress. He was also the social philosopher who was keenly sensitive to the crucial social, moral, and political issues of his time.

Comte caught, perhaps, a second glimpse of this ideal man when reading and meditating about Benjamin Franklin: the American hero who sought to become a perfectly wise man through clear thinking and hard work.

Comte further articulated his vision of the ideal man through his association with St. Simon. Through St. Simon, he became aware of the values and spirit of the time and realized that he was called to usher in the positive age through a spiritual regeneration and a social reconstruction. And, characteristically, this is the time Comte changed his name from Isidore to Auguste. From here, onward, all that happens to him, his sufferings, deprivations, illnesses, persecutions, and enormous labors, are providential, ordained by history and evolution to make him more capable of fulfilling his mission—to transform himself into the positive man.

Comte interpreted his "cerebral episode" of 1826 as but a "providential opportunity" for him to verify by personal experience the law of the three stages. Through this experience, the effects of his illness, and of poor medical care, he claimed that he descended through all the various stages of human thinking, to the theological stage, to then reascend later, during his convalescence, and reach again "positive maturity."

Comte's professional failures, the "conspiracy of silence" of the newspapers and scientists, and the ostracism of his colleagues are explained in terms of the struggle between the "ancien regime" of metaphysics and the "new world" of positivism, between the "old man" of metaphysics and the "new man" of positivism.

It is above all his encounter with Clothilde de Vaux, the "year without equal" he spent with her, and his great love for her that provided the final and crowning initiation necessary for him to realize and embody his conception of the ideal man. He, himself, acknowledged that "to become a perfect philosopher, I lacked above all else a passion, at once profound and pure, that would make me sufficiently appreciate the emotional side of humanity. . . . If you only knew the progress I have made in the last year in the midst of these apparent perturbations, towards my principal philosophical goal—the true systematization of the whole of human existence around its true universal center: love."[51]

It was through the initiation by love and by a direct, lived experience of what he had first conceived through his philosophical initiation that Comte "became" the ideal man, that he united with the great being. Clothilde taught him what love was at the experiential level; she therefore provided the living connection with the heart of humanity as St. Simon had provided the medium through which the Zeitgeist reached him.

With Comte's second career, the positive man reaches maturity and will become the priest of humanity. As Comte loved and united with Clothilde, who is the living embodiment of the great being, so the positive man must love humanity and become one with it. After his last initiation, Comte saw himself as the living embodiment of his conception of the ideal man and proclaimed himself, in 1848, the high priest of humanity. Living on a subsidy provided by some of his disciples, Comte set up his relationship with Clothilde and his personal life as the paradigmatic model for all men and all future generations.

Comte truly believed that he had not only a vision of the positive man of the future, but that he had actually become the living embodiment of it, which made his biographer, Gouhier, say that he had become obsessed by his system and his ideal. Thus, he wrote to politicians and heads of state, and even to dignitaries of the Roman Catholic church; he even said that he would institute a cult of Clothilde in the name of humanity, and that he would preach the religion of humanity in Notre Dame by 1861.

Comte's thought and intellectual system are clearly a projection and conceptualization of his ideal of the positive man and of his insight as to how persons could achieve this ideal. They represent the works and strivings of a man who seeks to know what man is and what man may become and should become; who finds and articulates this ideal in his intellectual system; who attempts to live it and to incarnate it, and, finally, to teach it and to pass it on to others.

In the first period of his social and political writings, Comte becomes sensitive to the great problems and issues of his time—mental anarchy, egoism, social and political confusion. Like his contemporaries, he seeks and proposes solutions: he seeks an ideal society, but only for the sake of an ideal man, whom he will project and hypostatize in humanity.

In the second period of his *Cours* and of his scientific-philosophical writings, which together form what he termed his first career, Comte seeks a theory of human cognition that will lay the foundation for a certain knowledge, for a positive knowledge that is universally acceptable. This he finds through his key insight: "All is relative," which he articulates and systematizes in the law of the three stages. Then, he develops his "classification of the sciences," the indispensable complement of the foregoing, to organize and integrate positive knowledge from all the various fields of human studies into one unified system. Having reached and systematized the last positive science, biology, Comte extends the spirit and the methods of the foregoing to the study of man and society and develops a social science—sociology. Sociology provides the perspective, the synthesis, and the tools Comte had long been searching for and striving to develop. Sociology means a shift from the objective method to the subjective method; humanity, rather than the world, is the unifying and integrating principle for the synthesis of positive knowledge. This shift enables Comte to further define and articulate his conception of the ideal man.

When Comte meets Clothilde and begins his third period, what he called his second career, that of the *Système*, of the *Catéchisme*, and of the *Synthèse*, he knows what man should become and how human society should be reorganized; but he has not yet experienced this knowledge. This is precisely what Clothilde brings to him.

> My angelic muse, after one year of objective influence, has now been for more than six years associated with all my thoughts as well as with all my sentiments. It is through her that I have at last become for humanity a double organ—an encyclopedic philosopher by the ascendency of the spirit and a Priest by the

ascendency of the heart. Without her, I could never have brought St. Paul's career to succeed that of Aristotle in establishing the universal religion upon a healthy philosophy, after having derived the latter from real science.[52]

The central insight of Comte's third period is that "one can tire of thinking and even of working, but that one can never tire of loving." Later he added, "great thoughts come from the heart;" love has a noetic value; love is the integrating and unifying principle in the psyche as well as in society. Just as his first fundamental insight gave him the foundation for formulating his law of the three stages, which served as the axiomatic basis for his theory of human cognition, so now this second insight of the primacy of love as the true integrating principle provided him with the basis for his theory of eudaemonia, the art of self-realization he articulated in his *Système*. Now Comte shifts from the "esprit de geométrie" to the "esprit de finesse," and he begins to live and to become the ideal he had at first merely grasped cognitively. As Manuel explains: "Since Comte conceived of himself as a symbolic embodiment of the man of the future, what was good for Comte, was good for mankind."[53] Here Comte and his system, Comte and his ideal man fuse and become one, and Comte himself becomes the paradigmatic model for the positive man of the future.

Toward the end of his life, Comte believed that he had indeed become the positive man, the "ideal man of the future," about whom he had dreamed in his youth, and that his work and life, his intellectual preparation and crowning love experience with Clothilde, had led him gradually to the realization and embodiment of this ideal. Now his mission was to communicate this ideal to others, to teach others how to achieve it. As Gouhier explains: "When Comte looks upon his mission, he sees it through the prism of contemporary history. His life becomes a chapter of his system: he is the elected one who must complete the work of Bacon and Descartes . . . and later of St. Paul and Charlemagne. . . . The system has devoured the man."[54]

In his *Système* and later in the few unfinished sketches of the second volume of the *Synthèse*, Comte further extends his conception of the ideal man by projecting, hypothetically, his vision into the distant future. Comte saw the natural sciences as a necessary introduction and preparation for the final science of morality; likewise, Comte's system allows for the development of science and technology only insofar as they contribute to the satisfaction of basic needs and to the ordering of human relationships—to the development of universal love and sympathy. In the distant future, man will be freed from almost all physical labor (since machines will do the work) and, therefore, from the related intellectual operations such work demands. After the ages of slavery, necessity, and labor, there will follow an epoch in which the intellect and emotions will enjoy the freest and fullest development. Then, and only then, will the distinctively human traits—love and intelligence—reach their apogee. Then, for the first time in human history, freedom from necessity will make possible the fullest development of pure consciousness, which is the essence of human nature.

At this point, the scientific culture, which is directly related to the demands of industrial activity, will come to an end; it will no longer be the focus and ethos of the culture. Esthetic and artistic work will absorb the energies formerly used for scientific and technical labors. Instead of devotion to the elaboration of scientific constructs and industrial works, people will seek the most direct means of self-expression, and they will find them in art and in the expression of emotions. Intelligence will then become fused with love and sympathy in a way that was impossible during the reign of science and industry.

In its youth, humanity was forced by natural necessity to labor to survive; thus it discovered and developed science and technology which freed it from this fatality. In the course of unfolding knowledge and activity, humanity will reach a point, at least in Comte's vision, where science and labor are transcended—where the essence of human nature will be free to express itself fully in beauty, truth, and goodness.

3

EMILE DURKHEIM

The Man, His Work, and His Sociocultural Milieu

Like Auguste Comte, whose work, ideals, and mission he reanimated, Emile Durkheim was an extraordinary man and yet representative of his time and country. He left a school of sociology behind him to continue his life's work and ideals, a few devoted and capable disciples, and a substantial number of seminal ideas and approaches which had a wide and profound influence in all the social sciences. In his native France, he made substantial contributions and opened the way for many educational and social reforms which took place in the twentieth century. He was, in short, a master to whom all students of human nature and of the nature of society owe a great debt; he set an example of the great humanist or, rather, of the genuine sociologist, and left behind him a promise and vision of great achievements to be undertaken by future generations of social scientists. Thus Robert Nisbet hailed Durkheim as the interpreter of an age; Durkheim rightly "identified the central themes of industrial and democratic society in the modern West" with great accuracy.[1] Jean-Auger Duvignaud, on the other hand, described him as the "indispensable initiator" and spoke of a "universal radiation of his thought."[2]

Durkheim was both a child of the Enlightenment and a man of the conservative reaction. He was a Frenchman of the second half of the nineteenth century and, more specifically, an intellectual of the fin du siècle. He integrates many of the heterogeneous and paradoxical cultural, philosophical, political, and social traits of France at the fin du siècle. These he sought, like his predecessor, Comte, to bring into consciousness and give a rational organization and expression. In his personality and work lie the deep intellectual and emotional imprints and reaction to the defeat of 1870, to the massacres of the Paris

46

Commune, and to the new but culturally anemic Third Republic, which had just begun to experiment with a new secular and democratic system of education and which has rightly been called "La République des Professeurs."

Nisbet, who has a profound understanding of Durkheim's character and of the relation of his work to his sociocultural milieu, states that there is an "ironic charm in Durkheim's relation to modern thought." Although a liberal in political thought and action, his sociology constituted a "massive attack upon liberalism." Although agnostic in religious matters, his sociology of religion is "perhaps the most convincing proof ever written of the functional indispensability of religion." Although thoroughly and explicitly committed to rationalism and science, the substance of his thought has "umbilical relation to the early nineteenth-century conservatism that had declared war on rationalism." Finally, although committed to a certain type of social engineering, the greater part of his work suggests the "near impossibility of any disruption of society's normal articulation of function, structure, and meaning."[3]

If Comte was the "last and, perhaps, the greatest of the Encyclopedists," then Durkheim could be depicted as the "first of the specialists" who strove to usher in the "age of specialization and of collective endeavors" in the social sciences and to inaugurate the new "sociological era." Durkheim worked tirelessly to differentiate sociology from biology and psychology on the one hand and from history and philosophy on the other. He developed appropriate methods and techniques for sociology and selected pertinent and manageable research areas and topics. As Félix Pecault once remarked: "Sociology which, in Comte, remains 'in the air,' in intellectual constructions which are not drawn from experience, it seems that Durkheim has solidly anchored it on the ground and inserted it in the conditions of science."[4]

Professionally, Durkheim was a professor turned sociologist and educator; intellectually, however, he was a philosopher who became a scientist in order to become a moralist and a saving prophet to his nation. Living in the age of science, which he saw, as Comte had, about to inaugurate the sociological era, his early philosophical and political interests, his great thirst for social justice, and his hunger for intellectual integrity naturally led him to science and turned him into a strict social scientist. His main objective was to formulate a rigorous theory of human nature and of the nature of society, and his ultimate aim was to provide a moral and ideological foundation for his country. Science, however, was not, for Durkheim, the end but, rather, the beginning, a means to an end which was philosophy, or knowledge, on the one hand, and morality, or the pathway to self-realization, on the other. Durkheim received both of his degrees in philosophy. He remained a philosopher throughout his life, leaving philosophy temporarily but returning to it when he was more equipped to make genuine contributions to it through his work in sociology.

Essentially, however, Durkheim was a moralist, the prophet of the new, secular morality destined to lead his country away from the impasse into which it had fallen after the scientific, political, and industrial revolutions. His profound, passionate, and lengthy search for truth, his quest for an analytical penetration into human and social reality by science, and a synthetic organization and interpretation of the facts and truths of the former by philosophy were, in fact, but a long and necessary preamble for what he saw as the essence of his life's work: the development and preaching of a modern, secular, morality, "la science des moeurs." Durkheim believed that this science would lead modern men to the individual and collective realization of their own being and to a regeneration of contemporary socity. Daniel Essertier, in his introduction to Durkheim's *Morale*, claims that it "was the goal of his existence" and "the heart of his soul." For him, Durkheim's life-long passion was the question of social justice, which was, then as it is now, a truly crucial social issue. Durkheim, he says, saw the disoriented individual break down the last bonds that united him with the traditional groups, turn upon himself and attempt to "live his own life" and to "do his own thing" only to end up anomic and confused.[5]

In his first book, *De la Division du Travail*, Durkheim diagnosed the ills of his country and, thereby, rendered explicit the fundamental aim of his life's endeavors:

> Our faith has become troubled; tradition has lost its empire; individual judgment has emancipated itself from the collective judgment. The remedy for this sickness cannot be looked for in the same traditions and practices which, no longer corresponding to the present conditions of the social state, could but live with an artificial and apparent life. Our anxiety springs from the fact that certain of these duties are no longer anchored in the reality of things, a confusion has resulted from all this which only a new discipline, once established and developed, will be able to end. In one word, our first and foremost present duty is to develop a morality.[6]

Durkheim is saying that modern societies have changed very rapidly and that man's essence, his humanity, is a product of society; thus modern man needs first of all a precise and objective knowledge of himself and of his sociocultural milieu. This knowledge he sees as indispensible and as his first objective; yet, by itself, this knowledge is not an end but a means to the true end, which is self-realization, the actualization of his humanity. This cannot be achieved by thinking and meditating, by knowledge and truth alone; it can only be achieved by living and acting in concert with one's fellowmen. Hence, today morality is man's greatest need and the ultimate end of science and knowledge. This fundamental truth was already perceived by Plato and Aristotle whose philosophies and epistemologies are grounded in ethics.

Durkheim was concerned with the problems besetting his society; most of his thinking and theories originated, in fact, as a response to the crucial problems and questions raised by his sociocultural environment. His entire work is a highly rationalized and organized philosophical meditation on his society and its needs, which he then universalized and systematized into a coherent system. As his sociology and its central premises indicate, the major focus of his preoccupations and interests lay outside of himself, in the society in which he lived and from which he hoped to glean insights and solutions.

Emile Durkheim was born 15 April 1858, in Epinal, a small town in the sprawling foothills of the Vosges. Durkheim's birthplace is a clue to two of his major lifelong character traits: his pugnacious and polemical spirit and his serious, methodical, and austere attitude toward all human problems and all the intellectual questions he approached. It is as if the spirit of northeastern France and of southwestern Germany had met in the young Vosgian and found an eloquent voice. His biographer, Georges Davy,[7] reports that Durkheim did not share the youthful ebullience of his companions; he believed that effort and even sorrows were more conducive to the spiritual progress of man than joys and pleasures.

The country into which Durkheim was born and which had a deep influence on his character and work has been described by Werner Stark. "Strife rent the nation from end to end, and individualism was rampant, above all among the educated classes and the academics. It was against this individualism that Durkheim fought. The polemical tone of most of his writings shows that his pen was not that of the detached scholar, of the dweller in ivory towers."[8] This is perhaps one of the reasons why Durkheim became a moralist.

The sociocultural milieu that formed Durkheim's character and thought contained sharp and fiery contrasts. In the provinces people lived pretty much as they had in previous centuries. Farmers and artisans still outnumbered urban and industrial workers, but the industrial workers were increasing daily and lived in conditions of dreadful poverty. The Paris to which Durkheim came to complete his higher education and to make his home was an intriguing metropolis for some and a frightful hell for others—a true microcosm of France.

The two major events that became the sociocultural axes for those of Durkheim's generation, and to which they reacted sharply in their works, were the defeat at Sedan in 1870 and the massacres of the Paris Commune, which followed. Moreover, a strange phenomenon took place at that time. While the country was slowly moving toward the left, toward republicanism, Paris swung to the right and became a "bastion of conservatism surrounded by a red belt."[9] The Third Republic officially came into being in 1875 and proved to be one of the most stable and longlasting of all French republics; it weathered many crises and scandals, chief amongst which was the Dreyfus Affair, which split the nation in two.

The Zeitgeist of Durkheim's age is depicted by Nisbet as marked by three major intellectual currents: analytical individualism, biologism, and the idea of moral progress. These three major currents formed Durkheim's intellectual perspective as he developed his sociological synthesis. To these, furthermore, must be added the impact of the Industrial Revolution and the French Revolution, as well as the influence of two intellectual traditions—positivism and conservatism.

Nineteenth-century philosophy, psychology, and ethics were steeped in individualism. As Nisbet points out, "reality was held to be, not in institutions or social groups, but in man himself—man the root, man the microcosm—and in the hard, unchanging intraindividual elements of which man was made."[10]

To Durkheim, who always stressed order and integration, this view was unacceptable, because if man is truly an individual, he could not adapt to a social order that negates the very essence of his being. This raised the Hobbesian question anew, to which Durkheim provided a fresh answer that has now become the foundation of one of the major schools of sociology. His central insight was that a complex system of institutionalized and internalized norms, issuing from a central value system, provides the fundamental core of social integration. As Talcott Parsons lucidly explains it:

> It became clear that the moral component of the *conscience collective* is society: First, in that it is made up of values that are common to, and shared by, the members of the society; second, in that through the process of socialization the new members of the society undergo a process by which these values are internalized; and third, in that there are special mechanisms which re-inforce the commitment to the values thus made in ways that involve

non-rational layers of the personality structure, so that deviation is counteracted by certain mechanisms.[11]

In other words, Durkheim's central intuition is that it is necessary to begin with society and not with man in order to understand social behavior. And society is to be conceived as a psychic reality sui generis rather than as a tenuous aggregation of persons held together by fleeting economic and social relations.

Closely following Durkheim's critical thrust against individualism, came his polemic against the philosophy explaining human behavior in terms of physiological or biopsychic processes, against epiphenomenalism and reductionism. The fact that two of the greatest intellectual giants of the age, Pareto and Freud, turned to biology or biologically-derived factors for the explanation of psychological, social, and cultural phenomena is a good indication of the profound inroads that this perspective made on the learned minds of this era.

From the beginning of his career, Durkheim had been interested in a theory of human nature; its formulation became a central aim in his sociological studies. Thus to the theories of the biological unconscious and of the psychological preconscious, he added that of the social and cultural subconscious. But, carried away by his own breakthrough and enthusiasm, he went too far in that direction and, in my opinion, violated one of his own fundamental principles: never to explain the higher by the lower, the superior by the inferior. He collapsed man's superconscious and sociocultural subconscious and thus explained the spiritual dimension in man by the sociocultural factors which he came to see as the very essence of man.

The Critique of Progress was Durkheim's third reaction against an ingrained premise of his age. Although greatly influenced by the Enlightenment concepts of "the infinite perfectibility of man" and of the "ever-greater conquests of science, technology and industry," Durkheim rejected them in the period of his mature thinking. Already in 1895, and particularly after having written *Suicide*, Durkheim became more critical of the prevailing theory of progress. He became increasingly pessimistic about the advantages of modern society. By this time, Durkheim was far less enthusiastic about the "liberating" and "beneficial" effects of modern society than he was worried by its resulting anxieties, insecurities, and dilemmas, by the anomie he saw resulting from the great modern conquests of secularism, industrialism, and urbanization.

Durkheim was profoundly affected, both at the cognitive and at the existential levels, by the Industrial Revolution and the French Revolution. Durkheim's sociological synthesis could, in fact, hardly be explained and understood outside of the disruptive effects of these transformations of European society. Modern sociology was born in the aftermath of these two revolutions and represents a supreme attempt of the human mind to understand and to explain the transformations which had been set in motion and which profoundly affected human lives and destinies. Sociology was an attempt of the human mind to create a new psychosocial cosmos; it emerged as the modern religion from the prophetic visions and hopes of those who fashioned its Promethean foundations.

Positivism and conservatism are the two basic intellectual traditions which Durkheim reacted to in the intellectual atmosphere of his age and which, though antagonistic in nature, he blended into his intellectual synthesis. Positivism can be seen as a philosophy and a methodology rigorously anchored in the rational-empirical approach; conservatism consists of a set of fundamental assumptions about man and society anchored in tradition.

Positivism stood in direct lineal descent from the Enlightenment, sharing its secularism, rationalism, and materialism; conservatism was a nineteenth-century reaction to the Enlightenment and the French Revolution. Durkheim grappled with both traditions and, seeing valid insights in both, sought to reconcile them and to integrate them, at different levels, in his own system.

Methodologically, Durkheim remained a rationalist and a positivist, fully committed to science as the most valid and fertile avenue for truth. Philosophically and ideologically, however, he became more and more attracted and, finally, convinced by the central ideas of the conservatives.

Another important clue about Durkheim's character and thought can be found in his ethnic affiliation and in the career that his parents had envisaged for him. Durkheim was Jewish, the descendant of rabbis and biblical scholars, and had been oriented toward the rabbinate. His rabbinical studies and vocation, however, were shortlived. Under the influence of a Catholic tutor, it seemed, for a while, that he would turn to Catholicism; but then he underwent a "mystical experience" and became an agnostic. Yet something remained. As St. Simon and Comte before him, Durkheim felt that he had a most important mission, almost a sacred mission, to fulfill—to provide the educational and moral foundations for the Third Republic. "Sociology was to create a solid base for the Republic." It would show what reforms are needed and it would provide the principles upon which order could be reestablished for France. Durkheim's sociology, Richter claims, "originated in his concern for the reconstruction of France."[12]

Durkheim acted, wrote, and spoke with the zeal of a prophet. As his ancestors, the prophets and visionaries of Israel, had discussed the great moral issues involved in the destiny of their nation, so now Durkheim lectured, wrote—in secular and scientific language—and admonished his students about the moral needs of their time and the destiny of their nation. His demeanor, his imposing mastery of facts and profound knowledge of the fundamental moral and philosophical issues of his age gave him the charisma of a prophet—the authority that goes beyond that of a sincere, learned, and dedicated professor. That Durkheim was conscious of his messianic strivings can be gathered from a comment he once made to Célestin Bouglé, who reported it in an essay: "One could deeply sense in him the ardor of a preacher. As we passed Notre Dame, this son of a Rabbi told me with a smile on his lips: 'It is in a Chair such as this one that I should have spoken.' "[13]

That Durkheim created this impression in others and brought them to see him as a prophet and as a revealer of a new quasi-religion can be gathered from remarks made by his friends and students. René Maublanc reports: "He knew that he had in him the traits of a prophet and a missionary; that he wanted to convert disciples to a doctrine and, through teaching and thinking, enable his students to fulfill their role in the social recovery of his country.[14] Likewise, Georges Davy says that Durkheim wanted to be more than a teacher, that he wanted to expound a doctrine and to gather disciples. Durkheim's faith endowed his thoughts and words with genuine "inspiration" which "gave to those who listened to him the impression that before them stood the prophet of a newly born religion."[15]

After doing well in his local schools, Durkheim entered the Ecole Normale Supérieure of Paris in 1879, at the age of twenty-one. At this time, the Ecole Normale Supérieure was the center of an intellectual life bristling with high hopes and visions for the future of France and of humanity.

> It is not an exaggeration therefore to say that a veritable philosophical renaissance was germinating at the Ecole Normale. The establishment of the Third Republic, less than ten years previously, had become a sort of signal for France's intellectual awakening. The clarion call of freedom had been sounded and some of the great minds of the country, like Renouvier, feeling

themselves liberated from the, to them, throttling and repressive Napoleonic Regime of the Second Empire, could now pursue their labors with revitalized energies.[16]

Some of France's best minds were teaching at the Ecole Normale, and it was probably there that Durkheim first experienced what he later called "an effervescent milieu," a social milieu in which great ideas, insights, and ideals are generated and spontaneously come forth, in which human consciousness is expanded and heightened, thus giving birth to what he saw as the highest and most human part of man. It is also while attending the Ecole Normale with Bergson and Jaures, Picard and Holleaux, that the major aims and objectives, which Durkheim pursued for the rest of his life, emerged. He now sought to develop and articulate a secular morality, a common democratic ideology, and a corresponding system of education which would rest upon a solid and well demonstrated scientific foundation.

Upon his graduation from the Ecole Normale in 1882, Durkheim decided to dedicate the rest of his life to the scientific study of social phenomena. As Davy recounts: "From this moment on, the course of his life was definitely set: he was to be a sociologist."[17] For five years, Durkheim taught philosophy at the provencial lycées of Sens, Saint-Quintin, and Troyes. Also, during that time, in 1885-86, Durkheim took a leave of absence of one year to continue his own studies partly in Paris and partly in Berlin and Leipzig. With his students, Durkheim revealed himself to be an excellent professor. He sought with all the knowledge at his command to form the minds of his students, to unfold their powers of analysis and synthesis, and to sensitize them to the "spirit of the times" and to the crucial issues and needs of their society. As Maublanc recounts:

> In one hour, he synthesized in a few formulae all the known systems of explanation of a debated question, bringing out a new synthesis—the sociological solution. Then, all those who listened to him, agreeing or disagreeing, felt obscurely that before them stood one of the great heroes of human thought, the equivalent of an Aristotle, or a Descartes, of a Spinoza, or of a Kant.[18]

In 1887 Durkheim went to the University of Bordeaux where a special course in social science was opened for him, and for the next thirty years he taught sociology and education, moving back to Paris in 1902 to teach at the Sorbonne. In 1898 Durkheim founded a sociological journal, *L'Année Sociologique,* of which he was the editor for twelve years.

It was this journal that provided the central focus for the friends and disciples of Durkheim as well as for his fellow social scientists; and it was through this periodical that Durkheim exercised a deep influence on the development of French sociology and on French intellectual history of the Third Republic. It was around this journal that, as Davy tells us, "a spiritual family was united by the common method and admiration for their master. They constituted . . . 'une petite société *sui generis*, le clan de l'Année Sociologique.' Durkheim created and maintained the spirit and the unity of this small society without tyranny and leaving to each member his full liberty."[19]

It was no doubt in this "petite société spirituelle" that Durkheim experienced again, as he had at the Ecole Normale and while teaching some of his best classes, the "effervescent milieu" of heightened social interaction, expanded human consciousness, and revitalized sentiments in which "ideals are created and reaffirmed," in which man comes into direct contact with the sacred—the very best of human life, thought, and feeling which he would later ascribe to religion. Moreover, it was undoubtedly while functioning in such effervescent milieus, that Durkheim began to see the "sociologist" emerge as his conception of the ideal man, of the man who, having internalized in himself the "soul of society," the *conscience collective*, would now transmit it and establish it in others.

At the time of the Dreyfus Affair, Durkheim, who had sided with Dreyfus, made known his views on the dignity of man and on the new cult of the individual, which he saw as the emerging cult of the industrial age.

> The individualism of Kant and Rousseau, that of the spiritualists, that of the Declaration of the Rights of Man . . . has become the very foundation of modern morality. . . . This human personality, the definition of which has become the cornerstone by which to distinguish good from evil, is considered sacred, in the ritual sense of the word. . . . It has something of that transcending majesty which the Churches of all times ascribe to their Gods; one conceives of it as invested by this mysterious property which creates a void around holy things, which hides them from profane contacts and which withdraws it from common circulation. . . . Such an ethic is not therefore simply a hygienic discipline or a wise rule of existence, it is a religion of which man is both the God and the faithful.[20]

He further explains and concludes:

> If man has a right to this religious respect, it is because there is

something of humanity in him. It is humanity which is sacred and worthy of respect, but it is not contained wholly in him. It is spread out amidst all his fellow-men. The cult of which he is both the object and the agent, does not address itself to the particular being he is and in whatever form it is incarnated. . . . Ultimately individuality, so conceived, is the glorification not of the 'Moi' but of the individual in general. Its motive power is not egoism, but sympathy for all that is human, a large compassion for all suffering, for all human misery, an ardent need to overcome them, to soothe them, and a greater thirst for injustice. . . .

Individualism is not only not anarchy but it is, henceforth, the only system of beliefs capable of ensuring the moral unity of the country. . . . Thus, if it is true that a religion is, in a sense, indispensable, it is no less certain that religions transform themselves and that the religion of yesterday cannot be that of tomorrow. What is most important, therefore, is to determine what the religion of today must be like. . . . And all concurs to show that the only possible one is the religion of humanity of which individualistic ethics is the rational expression.[21]

Durkheim had sought, at the beginning of his career, to free sociology, and particularly its method, from philosophy in order to anchor it properly in its own foundation. In his mature period, however, after twenty years of relentless efforts, with the *Année* well on its way and the era of specialization now established, Durkheim saw the possibility of realizing one of his fondest hopes: that sociology, having reached a more mature stage, might become the indispensable tool and complement for the solution of the great social and philosophical problems of humanity. For Alpert, Durkheim envisaged sociology as a social science leading "inevitably to a synthetic philosophy of man, of human nature and human society."[22]

Thus, Durkheim became a sociologist and an armchair ethnologist in order to penetrate into the core of human nature, to explain the nature and genesis of the human soul. What interested him above all was man, the man of his day in particular. He had undertaken his sociological and anthropological studies to be in a better position to understand and to help the Frenchmen of his day, toward whom he felt a social and moral responsibility. As a social scientist, his fundamental aim was to know man in order to guide him to the fullest possible realization of his humanity. His sophisticated theoretical and methodological developments are the logical consequences of his, at first, intuitive and later rationalized theory of human nature.

Thus man, for Durkheim, is essentially a homo duplex, a biopsychic and a psychosocial being. At the human level, people can be explained only by relating them to the social milieu in which they have arisen and where they must realize themselves. Moreover, the social influences acting on the individual and molding his soul are, for the most part, subconscious and unperceived by the individual himself, so it is only through an understanding of society that the psychosocial part of man can be known.

After the death of his beloved son and promising disciple, André, Durkheim fell ill and knew that his end was near. He began to rearrange his papers and manuscripts to make the work of those who would ensure their publication easier. On 15 November 1917, Durkheim passed away quietly, his mission being almost accomplished.

Durkheim's Theory of Human Nature and his Conception of the Ideal Man

Like Comte, Emile Durkheim was a scientist with a method, a philosopher with a system, and a prophet with a vision. His aim in life was to reconcile and integrate science, philosophy, and religion in a grand rational synthesis. He was a man of his age and his work reflects the inner turmoil, the deep contradictions, and the profound yearnings of his society; yet he was also a man ahead of his age who contributed substantially to the making of his nation's cultural orientation. Above all, however, and by his own admission, Durkheim was a rationalist with a quest for clear and distinct ideas, well organized and systematized, on the most abstruse problems of man and society. As Maublanc claims:

> Durkheimism is above all, unless I am mistaken, a positive justification of rationalism. . . . He believed in reason, he confessed his faith in reason and in its moral expression, duty, with the same intransigence and the same ardor as his ancestors, the Prophets of Israel, declared their faith in Jehovah. It is here that we find the roots for his positive explanation of reason.[23]

The sociological philosophy of Durkheim, as all great philosophical systems, is an attempt to explain man and his existential experiences in their totality. Its structure rests on a theory of human cognition just as its motivational impetus rests on his desire to penetrate to the bedrock of reality in order to lead man to the fullest possible actualization of his humanity, and to help his struggling nation to realize its promises and possibilities.

Durkheim begins with the idea that individual experience cannot explain all that which the individual finds in his mind. Empiricism in all its forms—sensualism, associationism, epiphenomenalism, and even pragmatism—cannot go beyond the sensible world. But Durkheim tries to account, scientifically, for the nature, origin, and dynamics of all those elements in human consciousness which transcend individual sensate experience without, however, having recourse to any transcendental explanations.

In short, the fundamental problem for Durkheim is to explain all that which the individual encounters in his consciousness which his individual experience is powerless to explain—the concept and language, duty and obligation, reason and the categories of the understanding, the idea of the sacred and of God—all that which appears to be transcendental while, at the same time, being immanent in man. What he seeks to find in the world of man's experience are the signs and expressions of a supraindividual reality, of a reality which, as Maublanc described it, "dominates the individual and which can, at times, constrain him, but of which he is an integral part and which he feels within himself as his own substance."[24]

This reality, for Durkheim, is not that of the spirit, but that of the group, which generates a synthesis of ideas and sentiments. This is to individuals what the chemical compounds are to their elements and the living organism to its cells. Durkheim casts in new terms and interprets through a new perspective, some of the perennial problems of philosophy, chief among which are the Platonic theory of knowledge and the Kantian ethic.

Durkheim gave a new interpretation to the famous distinction Plato drew in the *Republic* between the image of the world as apprehended by the senses and the image of the world as grasped by reason. The sensible image of the world he related etiologically to man's biopsychic nature; the intelligible conception of the world he related to man's psychosocial nature. Ideas, for him, are the product and reflection of man's social life, and the fundamental categories of human understanding are abstractions and projections of his primary social experiences.

Here is a clear and explicit statement of the basic relationship between Durkheim's theory of human nature and the rest of his philosophical system. Durkheim's philosophical, moral, and social theories rest on his central premise concerning man's nature: man is seen as a two-story house, individual and social, whose essence is psychosocial even though its substratum is biopsychic.

It is society, the conscience collective, that explains the a priori and transcendental elements of consciousness, as well as the traditional theological, metaphysical, and philosophical systems. It is society, but society seen as a reality that "overflows" into the individual from all parts, a reality infinitely richer and higher than our own and "interior to us as it can only live in us and by us." It is "in a sense our very self, but the better part of ourselves."[25]

Durkheim's life work, like Comte's a few decades earlier, is a masterful attempt to develop a science of man. It is an attempt to solve, through a new approach, the problem raised by Socrates: *gnōthi se auton*, the problem of the nature, genesis, principles, and self-realization of the sentient beings we are, which stands at the root of all humanistic philosophy.

Durkheim's work contains the same two *leitmotivs* that had animated the life of Comte and underpinned his intellectual system: a theoretical quest, a search for truth, and an expanded and heightened consciousness regarding the nature of man and of society; and a practical endeavor, a striving for self-realization and for the actualization of the highest human faculties and potentialities.

These two quests crystallized into his magnum opus, *La Morale*, a science of man and a science of morality which he never completed. The first flowered into a theory of human cognition leading to a sociology of knowledge that finally culminated in a true philosophical system. The second led him to a theory of *eudaemonia*, which flowered into a theory of moral education and programs for social reforms. Both were the fruit of long and precise studies covering a disparate array of topics, ranging from political economy to an interpretation of religion through a philosophy of history and theories of education. His intellectual system, resting on a theory of human nature, articulated a theory of the nature of society, of history, and a conception of its own scope and methods, which were clearly grounded in the former. Moreover, at the summit of Durkheim's theory of human nature stood his conception of the ideal man, of the good and fully realized man. For, although Durkheim's interests and strivings were primarily oriented toward gaining knowledge and understanding of the human and social reality, ultimately they went beyond these to the realization of the good man, living the good life, in the good society.

Although Durkheim's allusions to and fragmentary exposition of his theory of human nature are scattered throughout his entire work, the core of his theory can be found, in a condensed and explicitly articulated version, in one of his later articles, *Le Dualisme de la Nature Humaine et ses Conditions Sociales,* which appeared in 1914.

The central assumption of Durkheim's theory of human nature is that society fashions and organizes man's psychosocial nature, and, to know man, it is necessary first to know and understand the society which made man what he is at the human level. Social relations engender the personality in man and the positive science of these social relations, sociology, establishes moral autonomy. All that transcends and surpasses animality and biological life, for Durkheim, is of social origin. A human being is human only by living in, through, and for the social group to which he belongs; the collective life fashions and transforms his intelligence, moral conscience, religious beliefs, and idealistic aspirations, as well as the means by which they may be realized.

Durkheim's theory of human nature is grounded in a fundamental duality, that of the individual, biological, or animal being, and that of the social, moral, or spiritual being. This duality is the basis for Durkheim's theoretical explanations.

> In every age, man has been intensely aware of this duality. He has, in fact, everywhere conceived of himself as being formed of two radically heterogeneous beings: the body and the soul. Not only are these two beings substantially different, they are in large measure independent of each other, and are even in conflict. . . . It can be said that although the body and the soul are closely associated, they do not belong to the same world. The body is an integral part of the material universe, as it is made known to us by sensory experience; the abode of the soul is elsewhere, and the soul tends ceaselessly to return to it. This abode is the world of the sacred. Therefore, the soul is invested with a dignity that has always been denied to the body, which is considered essentially profane, and it inspires those feelings that are everywhere reserved for that which is divine.[26]

In the duality of human nature lie the fundamental characteristics Durkheim sees at the center of all religious and moral life, the distinction between the sacred and the profane, and the notions of authority and obligations. The religious beliefs of man, so profoundly rooted in humanity, cannot, says Durkheim, be purely imaginary; they must be rooted in reality, in a reality which, however, religions have hitherto expressed only in a vague and symbolic fashion but which the science of man will now explain rationally.

Human consciousness manifests this duality at its core. For Durkheim as for Comte, consciousness is both the essence of man's humanity and his highest and most distinctive characteristic. For both thinkers, it has three basic dimensions: intelligence, sensibility, and will. Each dimension exhibits this fundamental duality, the nature and consequences of which, however, have not been fully grasped.

Thus cognitive processes are subdivided into sensory impressions and conceptual thought; affective processes are polarized into egoistical and altruistic pursuits; and conative processes are characterized by obligation, or coercion, and by desirability, or attraction. Finally, social activities display an incredible complexity of antinomic drives and strivings which reflect the basic duality.

> Our intelligence, like our activity, presents two very different forms: on the one hand, are sensations and sensory tendencies; on the other, conceptual thought and moral activity. Each of these two parts of ourselves represents a separate pole of our being; and these two poles are not only distinct from one another but opposed to one another. Our sensory appetites are necessarily egoistic: they have our individuality and it alone as their object. When we satisfy our hunger, our thirst, and so on, without bringing any other tendency into play, it is ourselves, and ourselves alone, that we satisfy. Conceptual thought and moral activity are, on the contrary, distinguished by the fact that the rules of conduct to which they conform can be universalized. Therefore, by definition, they pursue impersonal ends. Morality begins with disinterest, with something other than ourselves.[27]

At a conference of the French Society of Philosophy, Durkheim asked: "Is not this aptitude to live an impersonal, supraindividual life, one of the central characteristics of humanity, perhaps that which best distinguishes it from animality?"[28] Finally, he concluded:

> These two aspects of our psychic life are, therefore, opposed to each other as are the personal and the impersonal. There is in us a being that represents everything in relation to itself and from its own point of view; in everything that it does, this being has no other object but itself. There is another being in us, however, which knows things *sub specie aeternitatis,* as it were, participating in some thought other than its own, and which in its acts, tends to accomplish ends that surpass its own. The old formula *homo duplex* is therefore verified by the facts. Far from being simple, our inner life has something like a double center of gravity. . . .

Not only are these two states of consciousness different in their origins and their properties, but there is a true antagonism between them. They mutually contradict and deny each other. We cannot pursue moral ends without causing a split within ourselves, without offending the instincts and the penchants that are most deeply rooted in our bodies. There is no moral act that does not imply a sacrifice.[29]

Durkheim, therefore, sees man as the *homo duplex* of the classical tradition, as an entity with two natures which, not having the same origin, do not have the same characteristics and the same orientation. Durkheim sees man as Pascal saw him, as "half beast and half angel"; or better still, as Hesse described him in *Steppenwolf,* as half an animal, or wolf, and half a human being, or man. However, Durkheim leaves out the true essence of man's being, which is spiritual and not biopsychic or psychosocial, and which is both the anterior source for them and the end to be consciously realized.

In conclusion, Durkheim conceives of man as a two-story house fully encompassed by nature and, therefore, open to scientific investigation and analysis. The first story of the house is the individual self, the biological organism, with its various biopsychic systems, faculties, and potentialities; it is basically a closed system which, differing in no essential way from those of other animals, has practically completed its evolution. The second story of the house is the social self which is fashioned and created by society and grafted, as it were, onto the first story. It is human consciousness, or man's capacity to know, to love, to will, and to act rationally and morally. Human consciousness is basically an open system, the conscious evolution of which is ever expanding and widening. Both the material contents and the framework of human consciousness are produced by social interaction and are of social nature and origin. Beyond these two stories there may be others, but, since they do not become manifest empirically in the collective human experience, Durkheim leaves them out at the price of, perhaps, doing precisely what he warned others against, namely, explaining the higher by the lower, the superior by the inferior.

In Durkheim's system, man's being is thus reduced to a physical body, or biological organism, and to a soul, or microcosmic and psychic reflection of society, which is purely psychosocial and which has nothing spiritual or transcendental in it. The soul is the product not of spirit or of nature but, rather, of society and social interaction. It is here that Durkheim's originality reveals itself, namely, in his conception that man's soul is not brought out, translated from potentiality into actuality, by human interactions and social relations, but literally created and fashioned by them, both in its specific cultural contents (for example, ideas, values, words) and in its very form or structure (that is, the categories of the understanding).

For Durkheim, because of his naturalistic bias, of his rationalistic tendencies to shed light on all the dark corners of man's being and life, and of his hypothesis of the creative synthesis resulting from the association process of lower elements, man's consciousness is explained by the only empirically observable reality which he could find, that is, by society. Society and history, therefore, are not, for him, the biography and the field of the unfoldment of human consciousness but, rather, they are various "factories" wherein different types of men are produced. Thus there is not one human nature, progressively unfolding and articulating its potentialities and faculties through the canvas of different societies and civilizations, as with Comte, but as many human natures as there are different types of societies.

Both Durkheim and Hobbes began with the same central assumption: that what is naturally given in man is egoism and asociality. For Hobbes, however, man remains essentially an egoistical and an asocial being, who can only live in society when social pressures and authority are strong enough to prevent a war of all against all. Only an egoistical calculus enables individuals to enter into contracts and exchange their absolute freedom of instinctual expression, which is the source of perpetual conflicts and sufferings, for civil peace and the pleasures of security offered by the Leviathan. For Durkheim, on the other hand, the socialization and moralization of an asocial and egoistical being, through education and social life, creates and fashions a new being in man that is both rational and moral, impersonal and universal.

Durkheim's fundamental premise, the cornerstone of his theory of human nature, is an unqualified and thoroughgoing naturalism. This premise led him to his dualistic view of human knowledge as consisting of sensations and concepts, and of human nature as consisting of a biopsychic and of a psychosocial being; finally, this premise, by logical extension, led him to conceive the highest part of man as a social product. Durkheim explicitly acknowledged his naturalistic bias. "We must redefine the moral forces which are at the base of all social life by forcing ourselves to find their rational expression. . . . And what is to find their rational expression but to make them enter the natural order of empirical phenomena and to make them the object of a positive science."[30] This "positive science," naturally, is sociology, which will, later, engender the "science des moeurs," morality.

Durkheim's conception of the ideal man is implicit in his work. A few allusions concerning this fully actualized man can be found from

De la Division du Travail to *Introduction à la Morale.* His works on education *(L'Education Morale, Education et Sociologie,* and *L'Evolution Pédagogique en France),* however, contain condensed and fully articulated visions of the highest human ideal.

Durkheim's conception of what man should become follows directly from his theory of human nature, which is anchored, on the one hand, in his naturalistic bias and, on the other, in his dual view of man as a biopsychic being and a psychosocial being. It is largely influenced by his theory of human cognition, that is, by his view of human knowledge and rationalistic strivings. It is the focus of both his theory of education and his theory of morality, whose aim is, ultimately, to produce the good society, which will produce the good man. His theory of human nature and his conception of the ideal man, moreover, underlie both his theoretical strivings for an expanded and illuminated consciousness, and his practical endeavors for a life more abundant.

For Durkheim, man as a human being was the "wonder of creation," the most precious of all treasures, and the most important of all mysteries on earth. Man as a person was, in fact, for Durkheim, the "last of the Gods" and the only object of cultural religion that remained in the modern industrial age. His vast and diversified sociological and ethnological studies were undertaken, ultimately, only to better understand man. His sociological and anthropological studies provided the necessary work to develop the science of man prefigured and demanded by Socrates.

It is difficult, because of a lack of pertinent materials, to relate the genesis and unfoldment of Durkheim's theory of human nature and of his conception of the ideal man to the formative periods of his life and to his most significant human relationships. Perhaps Boutroux played the role for Durkheim that Encontre had played for Comte and gave him the first glimpse and living encounter with the "good man"; and it could be that Renouvier or Hamelin helped him to crystallize it as St. Simon had done for Comte. Perhaps Durkheim also obtained crucial materials from his readings of Montesquieu, Rousseau, or Kant. These are difficult questions to answer and, at best, remain speculations.

However, it is possible to find the source of Durkheim's conception of the ideal man. It is directly related to, and in large part, drawn from, the general intellectual climate in which he lived. It is also an expression and crystallization of his own crucial life experiences and innermost longings. This conception of the ideal man is also organically related to and underlies the articulation of his entire intellectual system. It fitted his time and society, his personal experiences and character, and his own work and intellectual developments.

As in the case of Comte, Durkheim's conception of the ideal man and his entire intellectual system stood in a dialectical relationship to each other, mutually influencing each other. Moreover, Durkheim's theory of human nature, with his vision of the good man, overshadowed and oriented his theoretical and methodological developments, providing both the framework in which its basic materials could be organized and interpreted, and its general orientation and motivation; they led him to formulate the basic questions he asked and to structure, somewhat, the answers he gave.

In short, the central postulates of Durkheim's theory of human nature provided the framework in which his researches and theoretical and methodological developments were carried out. His vision of the ideal man, on the other hand, provided their axiological foundation and their higher unifying and integrating principle. The assumptions implicit in the former provided the preconscious, a priori, categories through which he worked, while the basic vision and premises of the latter provided the supraconscious drawing, motivating, and integrating power for them.

Durkheim's first explicit statement concerning what man should strive to become was made in the opening pages of *De la Division du Travail*. As the unfoldment of civilization and the foundation and emergence of the human personality rest on the division of labor, through its patterns of human interactions, and as the division of labor is now steadily increasing and differentiating, man should harmonize himself with it, he should specialize and further individualize himself and differentiate his faculties and capacities, and, thereby, increase his contributions to society. Moreoever, by selecting a well-defined and manageable area of endeavor, by specializing and becoming an expert in his own field, man should learn, concomitantly, to work less and less individually and more and more collectively, in cooperation with others. This follows logically from the first premise, because as man concentrates his work and contributions on smaller and smaller areas of a given domain, he will become more and more dependent on others to relate his work and contributions to the domain as a whole; moreover, he will become more dependent, for his own survival, on the work of an increasing number of people.

> The time has gone when the perfect man seemed to us to be the one who, being interested in everything and attached to none, capable of tasting and understanding everything, found a way of re-uniting and condensing in himself that which is most exquisite in civilization. . . .

We want that activity, instead of dispersing itself over a large surface, to be concentrated and gain in intensity that which it loses in extension. . . . The honest [ideal] man of the past is no more than a dilettante and we deny all moral value to dilettantism; rather, we see perfection in a competent man who seeks not to be complete but to be proficient in a limited task which he has chosen and to which he consecrates his life. . . .

Thus, the moral ideal which was one and impersonal in the past, now diversifies itself more and more. We no longer think that the exclusive duty of man is to realize in himself the qualities of the general man. . . . This is shown increasingly by the specialized character which education is now assuming. . . . Today, the categorical imperative of the moral conscience tells man: qualify yourself to accomplish a given function usefully.[31]

Logically implicit in Durkheim's first explicit statement of what modern man should strive to become, lies another fundamental assumption of his doctrine, namely, that if man is to gain expertise in a small and well-defined area of behavior and work increasingly more in team efforts, there is not one basic and concrete type of ideal man but many. This assumption is, in fact, both Durkheim's major criticism of the traditional conception of the good and fully realized man and the cornerstone of his own position. For Durkheim, the general error made by philosophers, metaphysicians, pedagogues, and even social scientists such as Comte and Spencer, was to assume that there was one fundamental human nature given ab initio, and that the central task of education, morality, and social life was to unfold and realize it.

This conception is erroneous, Durkheim tells us, because it was based on philosophical preconceptions and metaphysical speculations rather than on empirical realities revealed by history and sociology. Human nature, far from being homogeneous, fully defined, and integrated, is, in fact, highly heterogeneous, indefinite, and ever on the way to forming and crystallizing.

Durkheim was careful, however, to point out that as each society produces its own type of ideal man, it is not in the past but, rather, in the present, in our own society, that we should look for the clues to identify the ideal man of today.

It is neither in the Middle Ages, in the Renaissance, in the 17th or 18th century that we shall borrow the human model (ideal) that today's teachings must have as an object to realize. It is the men of today that one must consider; it is of ourselves that we must become conscious, and in ourselves, it is especially the man of tomorrow that one must seek to perceive and to unfold.[32]

Before elaborating Durkheim's conception of the man of tomorrow, I shall briefly review the three central features of the ideal man of today: he should specialize and individualize himself; he should learn to participate in collective endeavors; and he should learn that there is not one human nature and, therefore, one ideal to realize, but as many as there are societies and social milieus. These insights lead straight to the heart of his theory of human nature and to his conception of the good man. Namely, both man's distinctively human nature and faculties—knowledge, understanding, love, and the creative will— and his greatest values and ideals are the products of society, of the creative synthesis of human ideas, feelings, and strivings produced by human interaction.

Since Durkheim sees man as a purely natural being, as a two-story house composed of a lower biopsychic stratum and of a sui generis psychosocial superstructure, he logically infers that the psychosocial part of man and all of man's values and ideals can only be a product of society.

> The man whom education must realize in us is not the man such as nature made him, but such as society wants him to be; and society wants him to be such as its internal structure demands him. . . . Thus our pedagogic ideal is explained by our social structure, just as that of the Greeks and the Romans could only be explained by the organization of their City.[33]

In the past, human societies stressed courage and military virtues; today they prize thinking and reflection, and tomorrow they might emphasize refinement of taste and artistic sensibilities. In all cases, the virtues and ideals that educational systems stress are always, even in their smallest details, the work of society. For it is society that draws the portrait of the ideal man and this portrait always reflects its particular organization, structures, and processes. Education, therefore, for Durkheim, creates a new man or, rather, a new nature in man which constitutes his human essence, the best that exists in man, and which reflects the society in which he lives.[34]

Moreover, he reminds us time and again that:

> Social man necessarily presupposes a society which he expresses and serves. If it dissolves, if we no longer feel it in existence and in action about and above us, whatever is society in us is deprived of all objective foundation. All that remains is an artificial combination of illusory images, a phantasmagoria vanishing with the least reflection, that is nothing which can be a goal for our ac-

tion. . . . This social man is the essence of civilized man; he is the masterpiece of existence.[35]

For Durkheim, the ideal man of the present is the sociocentric person, whose social and moral nature has been fully realized, and who is capable of knowing and ruling the individual, or biopsychic nature. This conception closely parallels that of Comte, who saw the positive man as the man in whom altruism rules over egoism, in whom the love of humanity predominates over the love of self. The sociocentric man, moreover, is the man whose mind and soul are as full an incarnation and representation of the conscience collective as possible; thus, this person's psychosocial being is a microcosm of the social structure (in terms of its "categories of the understanding") and of the social life (in terms of its "sympathy" and "openness" to human relations) of his society.

It is the man in whom the greatest ideas, ideals, and values of his century find a full, conscious, and living expression; it is the man in whom his society and Zeitgeist recognize themselves, become conscious of themselves, and achieve the fullest possible level of self-expression. It is the man who opens himself to his sociocultural system, who welcomes and cultivates deep and meaningful human relations, and who gives of himself fully and freely to others, letting the moralizing and nourishing currents of his society flow freely through him.

The ideal person, for Durkheim, is the person in whom rationality has reached maturity and by whom the sciences have been fully mastered—what might be called a "modern Descartes." Society has entered this person and conferred a full humanity on him; science and rationality will now confer full moral autonomy to him as well. This person has clearly defined his ideals, that is, the collective ideals of his society, and he uses rational and manageable means to realize and objectify them. Therefore, this person has conquered "la maladie de l'infini," and knows what he wants; he has limited and contained his aspirations and desires.

In short, this person is content with what he is and what he has; he is fully adjusted to his sociocultural milieu and is in full harmony with the best of his Zeitgeist, being particularly senstive to its noblest and highest aspirations. This person's biopsychic organism has become a "temple," an instrument through which the "highest psychic reality," the "hyperspirituality" of society, can find its fullest and most conscious expression. This person is a "child of society" in the same way that the traditional man is a "child of God." Durkheim could well have said: "It is the man who loves society above all and who loves himself and other individuals only because of society, because of the incarnation of the conscience collective in himself and in others, which he can now easily discern."

Durkheim, in his insatiable desire and tireless efforts to explain all human mysteries in rational and scientific terms, identified the word God with the word society. He saw the substantial reality and distinguishing features of God embodied and expressed by society. Thus society is, in rational and scientific words, just as God was, in symbolical and metaphysical terms, both the source of life, which is to be loved as the highest good, and the legislator and disciplinarian, which is to be respected and obeyed. God, however, was not only the life-giving "mother" and the disciplining "father," he was also the "son" who had incarnated into, and expressed himself consciously through, people; he was the supreme model and ideal. Durkheim, therefore, extended his series of analogies and isomorphisms between God and society by seeing the sociocentric man as the supreme ideal for the good man.

> The Divine being was not only conceived as the legislator and guardian of the moral order. He was also an ideal which the individual sought to realize. To seek to resemble God, to merge with Him, such is the fundamental principle of all religious morality. If in one sense God exists and in the other He ceaselessly becomes, He realizes Himself progressively in the world to the extent that we imitate and reproduce Him in ourselves. Thus, He serves as the supreme model and ideal for man. This is because though He is infinitely superior to each of us, there is something in common between us: there is a Spark of Him in us which is the eminent part of ourselves which we call the 'soul' and which comes from Him and expresses Him in us. That Spark is the divine element in our nature which we must develop.[36]

Furthermore, in a later passage, he is explicit about how he identified the supreme being with society and established a system of analogies to represent, in rational, scientific terms, all that was attributed symbolically and metaphysically to a divinity.

> We all bear the divine imprint, the feeling which divinity inspires in us most naturally falls upon those who concur with us in realizing God. It is God that we love in them and it is under this condition that our love will have moral value. . . . We saw how we succeeded in expressing in rational terms all these moral realities; we only had to substitute to the conception of a supra-experimental being, the empirical notion of that being directly

observed which is society, not as an arithmetical sum of individuals but as a new personality distinct from individual personalities. We showed how society thus conceived commands us because it dominates us, and how it draws our will because, while dominating us, it permeates us. . . .

As the believer sees in the eminent part of his consciousness a Spark, a reflection of Divinity, we see a Spark and reflection of the collectivity. The parallel is so complete that, by itself, it already constitutes a first demonstration of this hypothesis, so many times indicated, that Divinity is the symbolical expression of the Collectivity.[37]

For Durkheim, therefore, the supreme model or ideal for man to realize and embody is the ideal put forth by his own society conceived as a "partial incarnation of humanity." Furthermore, as morality, which is the basic process by which man can accomplish and become his ideal, is grounded in duty or obligation and the good or desirability, two types of ideal men will emerge: the man of sentiment, sympathy, and enthusiasm, in whom predominates the aptitude of giving of oneself and of merging one's being, thoughts, desires, and will with that of the collectivity—the "mystic" of traditional theology; and the man of pure reason and will, colder and more austere, in whom predominates the sense of obligation and duty—the "ascetic" of traditional theology to whom Durkheim was, temperamentally, more drawn.

The "social mystic" and the "social ascetic" are thus, for Durkheim, the two moral models which emerge and bifurcate from his conception of the sociocentric man. As he tells us in his own words:

Two types of [ideal] men, corresponding to the two types of morality, oppose each other: the first have that self-control, that power of inhibition, authority upon themselves which are developed by the power of Duty; the others are characterized by that active and creative energy which is developed by a communion, as continuous as possible, with the very source of all moral energies, i.e., society.[38]

Underlying these two ideals, however, is a deeper and higher ideal of the man of today in Durkheim's system, one which integrated the former and which he, himself, sought to embody and to realize in his own life and work. This supreme ideal of man demanded by the state of modern civilization and by the spirit of the time, is that of the sociologist who will inaugurate the "sociological era."

Behind Durkheim's various conceptions and visions of the good man is the ideal of the sociologist as the modern and enlightened humanist and moralist, to which Durkheim entrusted his efforts and his life. In sociology his quest for truth and his strivings for self-realization meet and fuse. Sociology is to become a science of man, established on a firm and objective foundation; it is also from sociology that a science of morality can be deduced and elaborated. It is from sociology, therefore, that Durkheim asks for objective and systematic knowledge of human nature, of society and history, of the genesis and destiny of human powers, and of the means to unfold and realize them.

Sociology, the supreme science of the age, corresponds to the "intelligence of [the] time." Durkheim will seek to introduce sociology, with its particular conception of man, of the world, and of morality, into the French system of education as the modern synthetic discipline, or philosophy. Sociology will integrate the three crowning systems of human thought, science, philosophy, and religion by incorporating in itself the best of these three systems and will thus be the religion of the modern world; it will provide knowledge of the essence of human nature and destiny as well as the means by which to realize them. Sociology is the foundation for the philosophy of the modern era and the religion of humanity.

It is again in sociology that Durkheim found a proper harmony and expression for his scientific, humanistic, moralistic, and prophetic tendencies. The sociologist is the sociocentric man par excellence, because sociology contains the key to the most precious of human treasures: knowledge of man's nature, origin, and destiny, and of the sociocultural milieu which is the stage for the expression and realization of his being; moreover, it can unveil the means by which the social ills of the time can be diagnosed and cured, and by which man's essence can be actualized. Sociology, in fact, offers scientific knowledge to penetrate philosophical and existential mysteries, to explain and reconcile human dichotomies and existential antinomies.

Just as the natural sciences have made man the master of the natural world—by internalizing and understanding the laws and principles which govern its phenomena—sociology will make man autonomous in the moral world. It is from sociology, therefore, that an appropriate system of education can be developed just as an ethical system can be forged through its perspectives. Finally, it is sociology again which can reconcile the need not only for knowledge and self-realization, but also for specialization and individuation on the one hand, and for universalization and unification on the other; for reconciling and integrating duty and desire, coercion and aspiration, the individual and society.

In a revealing passage concerning the preeminence of sociology as a system of knowledge and, hence, as an ideal for a rational man who aspires to self-knowledge, self-mastery, and self-realization, Durkheim writes:

> It is inadmissible that the metaphysical problems, even the most audacious ones, which have preoccupied philosophers, could ever be forgotten. It is equally certain that they are called to be renovated; and, we believe that it is sociology, more than any other science, which can contribute to this renovation of philosophy. . . .
>
> Everyone, today, agrees that if philosophy is not grounded in the positive sciences, it can only be a form of literature. On the other hand, as scientific works divide and specialize more and more, it is evident that philosophy can fulfill its synthetic work only upon the condition that it possesses the encyclopedia of human knowledge—an impossible task. Under these conditions, philosophy has but one alternative: to find a science which, while restricted enough to be possessed by one mind, yet occupies a central enough position by rapport to the whole of human knowledge, to provide the foundation for a unified or philosophical speculation. Now, the sciences of the 'spirit' [i.e., sociology] are the only ones capable of satisfying this condition.[39]

The Ideal Man in Durkheim's Life and Intellectual System

At first, sociology appeared to Durkheim as a philosophical ideal, as the fundamental science of man's consciousness in the modern world. It was to reveal human limits and potentialities and provide self-knowledge and knowledge of the social world. At the same time, however, it also appeared to be the key to organize and develop morality—the way to self-realization, to achieving the fullness and perfection of one's being, and to find the badly needed answers to the most pressing social problems of his time.

Later, however, when this ideal began to live through Durkheim, it became his conception of the fully conscious, mature, and humanized man. It is to this ideal that he consecrated his life, or, at least, the best of his life—his last thirty (and most productive) years. All of Durkheim's life, in fact, was a quest, a quest for the holy grail of truth, of life more abundantly and consciously lived, and of the universal medicine for the contemporary ills of man's soul and of society. This quest led him to sociology which, in the end, became himself as he lived it. It is in sociology that Durkheim found first his ideal for truth, for human truth and reality, and then his ideal for action and realization, and, in the end, his ideal for man—for the man who had achieved the first and most important of truths, the truth or knowledge of himself, for the man who was on his way to realizing his humanity and his communion with society.

There is a congruence between Durkheim's theory of human nature, his conception of the ideal man, and his life and work. As with Comte, Durkheim's life and work were a long and sustained attempt at realizing and embodying his concept of the ideal man; and his intellectual system was, in fact, an intricate elaboration of the basic assumptions and insights of his theory of human nature and of their theoretical and practical consequences. Rather than postulating a causal relationship between his theory of human nature and his ideal for man, on the one hand, and his intellectual system and sociological theories on the other, I would say that they stand in a dialectical relationship to each other; they mutually influence, reinforce, and orient each other.

All the great Durkheimian concepts and hypotheses, in the background, bear his fundamental assumptions concerning human nature and, in the foreground, his vision of the ideal man. Thus, his theory of human nature provided the fundamental framework in which these concepts were proposed and developed, while his conception of the ideal man provided the motivating drive, the drawing energy of aspiration, and the integrating and unifying power of a true and lofty ideal.

Behind the key Durkheimian concepts of the conscience collective and of the creative psychic synthesis of human interaction stands his theory of human nature with its two stories: the individual biopsychic being, the creature of nature, and the psychosocial being, the creature of society. Behind Durkheim's theory of education and moralization lies his theory of the ideal man; education and moralization are the creation and fashioning of man's social and moral being, the incarnation of the social ideal, and the humanization and spiritualization of man's being.

His theories of the nature and dynamics of religion, of the origin and structures of knowledge, and of the genesis and function of the ideal are, once more, articulations and further developments of his theory of human nature, of how man's social nature acquires its human consciousness, its knowledge, and its ideals through the structures and dynamics of social life, as well as the means by which to unfold and to realize itself.

His theory both of suicide and of the need for strong social controls are further articulations of his conception of the struggle between the biopsychic and the psychosocial beings in man. His proposal of organizing occupational groups as the major moralizing and socializing factor in modern life, which would, at the same time, provide the required stability of the social system, bears witness to his theory of human nature. Human nature is fashioned and nourished by an active social life in a given social group, and the "occupational corporations" are the social groups that best answer the demands and needs of both modern society and modern man.

Finally, his science of morality and of man and society articulate his theory of human nature, that is, of the ways and methods by which to study it, to gather valid knowledge about it, and to guide it to its full realization and social expression.

Durkheim's vision and conception of the ideal man also motivated, inspired, and integrated all his efforts and researches, standing before and above them, as it were, at first blindly, perhaps, but then more and more consciously and rationally. Durkheim became a sociologist and consecrated the best of his life to sociology because it was the "sociologist" who appeared to him as the ideal man; sociology would lead to specialization, to engaging in team efforts, and to providing the most important knowledge—self-knowledge.

Now that religion has been superseded by science, for Durkheim, sociology will define the path to individual and collective self-realization, will show men duty and the good, and will explain and preside over the constitution of the moral personality and of the spiritual autonomy of man. Sociology thus inherits the task formerly assumed by theology, metaphysics, and philosophy, and the sociologist emerges as the ideal for modern man. In the new era, the sociologist is the illuminated, wise, and good man; whoever does not possess the sociological imagination is destined to remain in a state of intellectual darkness and moral heteronomy. According to Joseph Vialatoux, sociology, as conceived by Durkheim, is "a philosophy which directs and inspires this scientific enterprise and which, before the science is born, called it to realize and develop its principles and aims through appropriate methods, and which confers upon it, prophetically, its supreme human value and its unique claim to replace the obsolete values of the now obsolete metaphysics and religion."[40]

In his mature synthesis, Durkheim came to the conclusion that the master concept of his entire system, society, was neither a group of individuals, as the individualists claimed, nor an abstract metaphysical entity, as the philosophers had contended; nor was it a "social mind," as many critics had alleged but, rather, society was the common value system shared by a given population that gives them their identity and unity and ensures their common life.

> A society can neither create itself nor recreate itself without, at the same time, creating an ideal. . . . The ideal society is not outside the real society; it is part of it. Far from being divided between them as two poles which mutually repel each other, we cannot hold to one without holding to the other. For a society is not made up merely of the mass of individuals who compose it, the ground which it occupies, the things which they use, and the movements which they perform, but above all it is the idea which it forms of itself. It is undoubtedly true that it hesitates over the manner in which it ought to conceive itself; it feels itself drawn in divergent directions. But these conflicts which break forth are not between the ideal and reality, but between two different ideals, that of yesterday and that of today, that which has the authority of tradition and that which has the hope of the future.[41]

The great ideals, moreover, contain not only the secret of the social order but also the blueprint for the unfoldment and realization of man's personality; they contain the highest forms of psychic activity, or human consciousness, which Durkheim termed "hyperspirituality" and which he saw as the true essence and substance of humanity. Thus he came to see society as the creative psychic synthesis of these ideals, as the "holy thing par excellence," as the supreme being, or God; and, later, he conceived of sociology as the science of the ideal, the matrix for a scientific morality. Durkheim understood the tremendous importance of values and ideals, not only for the social system but for the individual as well; he regarded them as the substance and sine qua non for the existence of social life and, therefore, for the formation of the social being in man, for the humanization and realization of man. That is why he was so keen on developing a "science of ethics," a systematic and rational approach to the nature, genesis, unfoldment, and dynamics of ideals and values which constitute the essence of both man and society, and the "holy thing par excellence."

Durkheim understood that men needed ideals far more than they did bread or material comfort, which is why he claimed that the real poverty of his nation, like that of ours today, is not an economic but a moral poverty; our first and most important need is not to bring about more material well-being but, rather, to forge the soul with a morality appropriate to modern industrial societies. Durkheim never claimed that science could create ideals or values, as many of his critics assumed; only the creative psychic synthesis of interacting individuals can do that, but science should study the nature, development, and dynamics of ideals in order to favor the social conditions which would bring about new ideals—when these are needed—and which would reaffirm them and revitalize them from time to time.

Although the naturalistic atmosphere of his time and the scientific bias of his education blunted Durkheim to the deeper spiritual essence and potentialities of man, his profound interest in and devotion to man, coupled with a keen sensitivity and an incisive intellect, led him to grasp some of the more intricate dynamisms of human becoming. If, to the scientific and humanistic ideal of Durkheim's sociologist, we add the "mystic" of Bergson and Sorokin; if to Durkheim's theory of human cognition, based on empiricism and rationalism in a social context, we add the "intuition" and "inspiration" and the "spiritual dimension" of Bergson, Jung, and Sorokin, then we shall have a discipline capable of explaining man and his existential experiences in their totality, as well as a genuinely ideal man. But this will substantially alter both Durkheim's overall intellectual system and some of his central assumptions and insights regarding man's nature and destiny. And yet, this is precisely what Durkheim called us to do.

Man is the highly complex and intricate being, the "bundle of desires and contradictions," that Durkheim believes him to be, and the human dimension is the most profound and multifaceted of all realities. But man is also, in his depths, mostly unknown to himself, and the human dimension still remains unfathomable. When we push our investigations of it further, we come upon the threshold of the spiritual dimension. This dimension is the true essence of man; it is more complex and "unknown" than the biological unconscious, the psychological preconscious, and the social and cultural subconscious. Here we come upon the threshold of the spiritual superconscious which, indeed, seems to hold the greatest promise of the future and the most fertile avenue of exploration. A science of man and a science of morality, a systematic and objective knowledge of what man is and of what man can and should become, is still as important for us as it ever was to any generation and to any society, but it still remains to be accomplished at higher and deeper levels. But now, it seems to be aiming more toward traditional "wisdom" than toward the "science" of the eighteenth and nineteenth centuries—at least for those of us in whom burns unquenchable the great humanistic quest, the eternal enigma of the sphinx and the perennial Delphic injunction!

4

VILFREDO PARETO

The Man, His Work and His Sociocultural Milieu

Unlike Auguste Comte, Emile Durkheim, and Max Weber, Pareto was not the interpreter of his age and the prophet of the coming age; he was, rather, the critic, the debunker, and the frustrated thinker who reacted against the society in which he lived. He was frustrated in most of his practical endeavors and ambitions, humiliated and defeated in his most cherished ideals and visions, and eventually he left the active world for a contemplative life he could well afford. He withdrew from his native France and Italy to seek refuge on the quiet shores of Lake Geneva; he opted to live the life of a sybarite and to dwell among his angora cats rather than amid human beings, whose nature, behavior, and actions he sought so passionately and persistently to understand and to explain.

Had Pareto not been so caught up and driven by his own thwarted emotions and unrealized ideals, he would have been the objective and impartial observer of society and human behavior he claimed to be. But there was more Pareto in his works than social phenomena, more camouflaged passion than impersonal observation and analysis, more ideology than science, and more physics and mechanics than genuine sociology.

Pareto did gather an array of social and historical facts, but the categories used to classify and interpret them were his own. They were those of the "solitaire de Celigny," who had fashioned them and tinged them with the precipitates of his own unusual life experiences and temperament; they reflected an enormously passionate and frustrated nature, which had sought in vain to realize itself through action and which now sought refuge and expression in an impersonal and nonemotional science. They contained all of the cravings for action,

77

and for one's realization, which had been transposed into reflection and observation; they contained an aborted awakening and development of a human nature which had returned with an intellectualized impetus toward its biopsychic levels.

It is particularly in his choice of social data that Pareto's gargantuan biases and intellectual myopia are revealed; he focused on that tiny band, in the vast and complex arc of sociocultural reality, that corresponded to what was alive and vibrating within his own soul. Unaware of this fact because of a lack of self-knowledge, of love, and of sympathy for what he studied, Pareto merely projected onto the social and historical world his own idiosyncrasies.

Ultimately, Pareto's major sociological works, *Les Systèmes Socialistes,* and the *Trattato,* are far more an indirect projection and study of Pareto's life than they are an analysis and explanation of social systems, ideologies, or human society and human behavior.

Interestingly enough, Pareto claimed, as I do, that all investigations of society and history, of the structures and dynamics of the social system, and of the motivations and principles of social action, must rest on a theory of human nature—on an anthropology and, more specifically, on a psychology. This is one of Pareto's greatest and most substantial contributions to the social sciences. For him, therefore, all the social sciences and every sociological investigation must, ultimately, rest on a conception of man. Moreover, Pareto showed us that all the elements of the social system are mutually related; a person's work, intellectual universe, conceptions, and ideals are intimately related to his personal life and the intellectual atmosphere of his society.

Deeply influenced by Nietzsche's concept of the superman, Pareto saw the masses forever remaining in the quagmire of ignorance, superstitions, and delusions, the slaves of forces they neither understood nor controlled; thus they are the easy prey of elites using force or cunning. Although Pareto believed the masses did not and could not gain true knowledge and understanding of themselves or of the dynamics of society, he thought that he could and actively set out to do so.

In his youth he had internalized, to a large extent, the liberal, democratic, Mazzinist ideals of his father. In his mature years, however, after he had become bitterly disenchanted with the former, he turned more and more, at least for himself, toward Nietzsche's ideal of the superman, the lone great man who has wrested the secret of his own nature and who has the courage to look at reality in all its inhumanity and cruelty. For the ideal of his youth, Pareto substituted an antidemocratic and elitist concept of the "enlightened strong man," who rules those who remain weak and in darkness, and he adopted Nietzsche's distinction of "slave morality" for the masses and of "master-morality" for the few who had risen above the common herd. Since human nature remains much the same, unchanged and unchangeable, throughout history, all notions of a true ideal man are impossible. Therefore, Pareto eventually withdrew from all active participation in the world, not caring (at least in words) whether he was listened to or not, to live as a disillusioned spectator and recluse. His system told him that he did not stand a chance to realize any ideals, particularly that of a good man.

Pareto was also a grandchild of the Enlightenment, an offspring of the romantic and reactionary movement which rebelled against the ideals and visions of the Enlightenment, and, above all, he was disillusioned by the fin du siècle. Pareto, the scion of an educated and noble Italian family, was far too perceptive, sensitive, and intellectually keen to have been contented with luxuries, pleasures, and a materially comfortable life. He needed ideals to strive for and to realize; he needed a lofty vision and a worthy cause to which to dedicate his life and the best of his energies.

Deep down, in the inner recesses of his being, he had a deep thirst for justice, meaning, and purpose. The tragedy of his life, reflected in his works, is to have sought those ideals without being able to actively realize them. He sought meaning and purpose, beauty, truth, and goodness in the wrong direction, and, ultimately, this led him to disillusionment, skepticism, and nihilism. He sought them first in science and then in business and industry and, finally, in sociology, in a vision of human nature, human society, and human interactions stripped of all idealism, nobility, and deeper meaning.

The one direction and dimension that could have brought him the answer to his most pressing questions and the fulfillment of his deepest needs, he utterly neglected and discarded. Pareto had no use whatever for spirituality and saw all religions as nothing but a fabric of ideologies, superstitions, and self-delusions, indispensable for the integration of the social system and the personality system. Although he recognized religion's functional importance and indispensable "social utility," he rejected it for himself, seeing himself as having risen above its childish mythologies and sentimental tales, which he did not fully understand. Perhaps, at times, he wished he could have believed in a religion and have been comforted by its promise of ultimate justice, meaning, and hope. But his intelligence and profound erudition made that simple faith impossible. As Pareto could not realize his ideas, ideals, and ambitions in his own life, he projected this experience of personal failure onto his intellectual system, and disowned all ideals, replacing them with irrational biopsychic drives; he replaced justice with brute force, optimism with pessimism, and faith with a thoroughgoing skepticism and cynicism.

Pareto was born in 1848, the great year of liberalism, in Paris, "la Ville de Lumière et de Liberté," which was at that time the center and root of republicanism. He died in 1923, ten months after Mussolini's march on Rome and the triumph of fascism in Italy; he died in Celigny, Switzerland, which could well be called "mon repos," a haven of quiet and peace on Lake Geneva, well protected from the political, social, and ideological storms that raged over Europe.

The Zeitgeist of the age in which he grew up was characterized by an antithetical intellectual current. On the one hand, there was a belief in social and material progress, in the powers of reason, in the possibility of human perfectibility, and in the advances and conquests of technology and industry; and on the other hand, there was a growing realization that technology and scientific progress were not equivalent to social, moral, and human progress. Reason might, after all, prove to be an ephemeral and evanescent light beneath the surface of which lay more elementary and powerful forces—the emotions and the sentiments. Human nature might not be so readily amenable to enlightenment and improvement; the advances of technology and industry might, in fact, benefit only a small minority at the expense of a new and more hopeless form of oppression of the masses.

By the end of the nineteenth century, all theories of progress, the faith in reason, and the perfectibility of man were under strong attack. Pessimism was slowly but inevitably replacing optimism, rationalism was strongly undermined by the discovery of the psychological and social unconscious and by a concentration on human irrationality; discussion and moderation were being supplanted by an appeal to violence and to radical solutions. The tenuous liberal-democratic compromise was split apart by a strong radicalization and polarization on the left and on the right throughout Europe. By the fin du siècle, a profound psychological, philosophical, and political transformation was underway.

> It was a period of over-ripeness, of perverse and mannered decadence—the end of an era. . . . Unquestionably the major intellectual innovators of the 1890's were profoundly interested in the problem of irrational motivation in human conduct. They were obsessed, almost intoxicated, with a re-discovery of the non-logical, the uncivilized, the inexplicable. But to call them 'irrationalists' is to fall into a dangerous ambiguity. It suggests a tolerance or even a preference for the realm of the unconscious.

The reverse was actually the case. The social thinkers of the 1890's were concerned with the irrational only to exorcize it. By probing into it, they sought ways to canalize it for constructive purposes.[1]

The Italian regime, a poor caricature of the French Republic, was torn by even more violent political passions than France; it was tottering along in the wake of political and economic scandals, and of a cynicism, greed, and exploitation that were even more transparent.

The political, social, and economic crises of the liberal-democratic regimes of Europe, however, were only the surface expression of a much deeper crisis. Man's entire intellectual edifice, his conception of himself, of human life, human knowledge, and human destiny was rocked to its foundations. The fundamental world view introduced by the Renaissance, which had flourished during the Enlightenment, had now reached maturity, but had not yielded what had been expected. At this critical juncture in the history of Europe's intellectual development, two fundamental alternatives presented themselves: a return to faith, to spiritual and transcendental values, which had been discarded by the Enlightenment, or a plunge into skepticism and the law of the jungle.

A minority turned toward the first alternative, with Bergson at their head, while the majority, with Freud and Pareto at the forefront, chose the latter, being determined to draw the ultimate logical conclusions of the values of the Enlightenment.

The newly risen skepticism, with its other face, pessimism, now crept into all the fields in which faith in reason, in man's science and will, had formerly reigned. The nature of the social sciences, the impregnable fortress of rationalism and empiricism, was now being questioned, both as to its scientific validity and as to its social utility. Many new interpretations of man and life appeared. Starting from different viewpoints, and working with different methods and concepts, the critics of the old Weltanschauung now converged on one central core. To this core many labels have been given—irrationalism, antirationalism, antipositivism, the revolt against reason, neoromanticism, and so on.

The best label to apply to this core, I feel, is "anthropocentrism" or "subjectivism," because thinkers like Freud, Sorel, Weber, Bergson, and Jung were beginning to realize, independently of each other, that knowledge of man is the prior condition to gaining knowledge of anything else. Thus they realized, each in his own way, that man is the ultimate instrument, the prism through which all knowledge and understanding flows and, therefore, that man had to be known and understood before the scope of knowledge could be ascertained.

The central thrust of the Enlightenment, and of science in particular, had been to focus on the objective world; thus the laws of physics and mechanics, of biology and physiology, of economics, politics, and sociology were developed. These were all implicitly assumed to exist outside and beyond the observer, to be independent of his personality and whims, and to reveal the texture of reality.

Now, however, critics and thinkers of the fin du siècle, their faith in reason, progress, and science shaken, began to ask themsleves the fundamental questions: How do we know that these laws are true laws, that is, objective, impersonal, and universally valid? By what processes do we actually derive these laws? What is their true scope and validity?

The conclusion to which most thinkers came is that laws are human statements about the external world and that, as such, they are necessarily influenced and conditioned by man's psychic makeup and orientation, which now becomes the center of interest. In the laws of science and positivism, personal elements had been abstracted or discounted altogether. Once the personal element is taken into account, however, these laws no longer appear so objective and impersonal; they now appear to be, to a large extent, subjective molds man himself has fashioned in order to come in contact with and to investigate reality. The subjective element is now being focused on and is considered vital for a proper understanding of man, of the world in which he lives, and of his actions in the world.

Up to the end of the nineteenth century, most scientists assumed that all natural phenomena could be reduced to the laws of mechanics or to the laws of biology, and that science, therefore, could predict the future course of the world, of humanity, and of human society. The discovery of non-Euclidian geometries, of radioactivity, of Einstein's theory of relativity, and of quantum mechanics brought back into question the nature and the validity of the so-called scientific laws of nature. In the social, political, and psychological sciences a similar reaction took place. Freud, Bergson, Weber, Durkheim, and Pareto, who were all members of the same intellectual generation, growing up under the same Zeitgeist and reacting to it, provided intellectual answers to these questions, each in terms of his own personal experiences and intellectual system.

Thus Freud came to see most of human behavior as a sublimation and projection of biopsychic drives and complexes buried in the unconscious. Bergson came to see reason and science as inadequate for explaining the dimensions of reality involving life and man in particular; only "sympathetic communication" between the subject and the outer world could yield true knowledge and understanding of reality, which could not be established by the intellect but only by the creative intuition. Durkheim came to see society and its culture as an externalized "collective representation" of social ideals and values, and it was those collective representations, those common values and ideals, he argued, which had fashioned our categories of the understanding through which, in turn, we could know and understand society and ourselves. Weber came to the conclusion that the social sciences had to develop their own distinctive methods of research, in addition to those furnished by the natural sciences. These consisted essentially in the verstehen approach, that is, the development of empathy between the subject and the object he wishes to study—if the objects in question are human beings. In America, William James asserted that truth was not an objective and fixed measure but, rather, that it was essentially a subjective criterion that changed and unfolded according to its usefulness to the subject who had conceptualized it.

Pareto was ten to fifteen years older than either Freud, Durkheim, Bergson, or Weber but, as his sociological vocation developed late in his life, he began to articulate it about the same time the others had already developed their own work (in the 1890s). Like the other members of his intellectual generation, Pareto had sensed, and later stressed to unfortunate proportions, the intrusion of his own personality and temperament into the framing of what had, hitherto, been viewed as strictly objective laws established by the naked intellect and the unadulterated senses.

Pareto's life can be roughly subdivided into three main periods: his youth and adolescence, which were spent in Paris and in Turin; his formative adult years, spent in Rome and Florence, during which he underwent his crucial life experiences and crystallized the fundamental premises of his intellectual system; and his mature academic and scientific years, spent in Celigny, teaching at the University of Lausanne and writing his major works.

During his first period, Pareto acquired his education, his love of classical literature, and his strong scientific bent with a mechanistic model of equilibrium at its heart.

During the second period, Pareto launched himself in an active and politically committed life; he tested out his ideas and ideals, failed in most of his practical endeavors, and saw his most cherished ambitions repeatedly frustrated. During this period his personality crystallized and consolidated itself; he acquired the axiological foundation of his thought; and he developed his most fundamental insights. His theory of human nature also began to emerge and he gave up most of his earlier ideals concerning man and his destiny; the absence of a conception of an ideal man into whom everyone could develop came to the foreground.

During the third period, Pareto retired from an active political and economic life; he renounced being an involved and concerned actor on the stage of Italian society to become a professor and a spectator, a critic of human follies and superstitions. He was abandoned by his wife, who left with his cook and with a good part of his possessions and sought to extract as much money from him as she could until the end of his days. This was the last of his great disappointments. Thereafter, he devoted most of his affection and concern to his angora cats and his mammoth Voltairian works, being thoroughly disillusioned about life and human nature, and, perhaps, about all human endeavors except those of science and the pursuit of the culinary arts.

Around 1854-55, Pareto's family returned to Turin and Vilfredo attended the local *lycée* and, later, the Polytechnical Institute to pursue the same career as his father. At the *lycée* he did classical studies, and while at the university he specialized mainly in mathematics and physics to qualify himself for a degree in engineering. As his biographer, George Bousquet, put it: "His entire work bore the imprint of the double influence of the Graeco-Latin humanities and of mathematics and physics."[2]

Upon graduation, Pareto began his career as an engineer and entered into the second crucial period of his life. From 1870 to 1874, he was the director of the San Giovanni Val D'Arno Railways and, thereafter, the general manager of the Societa Ferriere d'Italia. In Florence, a city whose atmosphere and social climate was more conducive to a worldly life and to the passions of politics than to the advancement of science and the flights of philosophical idealism, Pareto sought to enter the political struggle. Busino recounts:

> He believes that the fact that he is an engineer and that he has mastered sophisticated mechanical techniques will suffice to open the door of the ideal club in which reside those who control the destinies of the country. Very soon, however, he realizes that neither his competence nor his zeal are sufficient: the magnates of politics and the knights of a nascent industry are not easily impressed by his degrees, quite on the contrary, they are against those people—rare at that time—who preach parsimony and who judge severely the lack of scruples and the veniality of politicians.[3]

In 1882, Pareto presents himself at the legislative elections in the district of Pistoia as an opposition (liberal) candidate. He was badly defeated and remained psychologically and ideologically crushed by this political failure, which he compared with Newton's electoral failure. From the pacifist, humanitarian, and idealistic activist he was, Pareto now becomes more and more antihumanitarian and cynical. This is a fundamental turning point in Pareto's life. "I do not have the slightest chance to ever be anything in Italy. . . . I do not hope for anything and I do not fear anything, for he who is already on the ground can never fall. Thus, I look upon everything from an objective viewpoint and never from a subjective viewpoint, at least so it seems to me."[4]

This passage summarizes the political and psychological drama of Pareto. It reveals an embittered and frustrated idealist, a passionately proud man, whose spirit and ideals were broken and who sought refuge in a haven of contemplation and reflection far removed from the practical affairs of life. He had imagined that he would look at social reality objectively and scientifically, without feelings or preconceptions. At this time he also began to see the Italian government as a group of "politicasters" using political power and pressure-group tactics to win economic favors as well as using economic power to win political success, but concealing all these machinations behind a facade of democratic elections and progressive legislation. "Now the condition of our fatherland is such that all liberty, except that of the politicians, has vanished; all has been attempted to abolish, in the popular conscience, any honest and righteous feelings."[5] He concluded: "To live in this country, one must be either a thief or a friend of thieves."[6]

It is from such experiences that Pareto's skepticism and cynicism issued. As a result of his frustrated political aspirations and unrecognized economic talents, Pareto took flight from the world of human affairs, which he had hoped to shape according to his vision and ideals. As his practical adventures and experiences in economics, industry, and politics did not turn out brilliantly, Pareto later became convinced that the world was evil, that power is always corruption and exploitation, and that men are always perverted by it.

When his father died in 1882, Pareto took his mother to live with him, and when she died, in 1889, he changed his entire way of life. He married a penniless Russian girl from Venice, Alessandrina Bakunin, and retired with her to the Villa Rosa in Fiesole. Pareto never recovered from his political defeat and became increasingly convinced that his political and economic views did not have a chance in Italy.

Through the mediation of his friend, Pantaleoni, Pareto succeeded Walras in the Chair of Political Economics at the University of Lausanne, becoming in 1893 an assistant professor and, in 1894, a full professor. This event marked the beginning of his scientific career and was another crucial turning point in his life.

In 1898, Pareto inherited a substantial sum of money and bought the Villa Angora in Celigny where he settled for the rest of his days. First place belonged to Pareto's twenty to thirty angora cats; they roamed freely about his house. He personally prepared their food and enjoyed feeding them. At the Villa Angora, cats were usually served before human beings according to the explicit orders of the master.

In 1901, Pareto went to Paris to deliver a lecture while his wife was to go to Russia to visit her mother. On his return to Celigny, he discovered that she had left, but neither alone nor empty handed. With her went the cook, who had become her lover, and thirty trunks of luggage and furniture. Pareto immediately began legal action against her, but he only succeeded in divorcing her sixty-one days before his death in 1923, after a long and bitter financial struggle. This negative experience further reinforced the germs of his hatred of humanity which, henceforth, was to dominate both his character and his works. These life experiences provide the key to Pareto's philosophical anthropology.[7]

The central premise of Pareto's intellectual system now becomes the following: the true social scientist, or student of human nature and of the nature of society, must penetrate through the subjective layers to reach the objective aspects of human actions and social phenomena; he must go beyond the ideas and reasonings that an actor has formed about his behavior to the hard core of the reality of his actions and of their implications. In other words, all sociological investigations must begin with an investigation of human nature and of the unfoldment of man's personality.

For him, the social sciences are, henceforth, to be based on a psychology, the rudiments of which he will endeavor to develop later on. It is up to the psychologist to study the different psychic forces that converge in the act and to see how these forces determine man's will, which, in turn, determines his actions. And it is up to the sociologist to study and classify these overt actions.

The core insight of this psychology is that most of human behavior is, in fact, nonlogical; logical actions depend essentially on reasoning, but nonlogical actions depend on psychic states he called the "residues." "Men call voluntary acts which are not voluntary, logical actions which are non-logical and strangely draw from their imagination the reasons by which they deceive themselves and others concerning the real causes of their own behaviour."[8] From this key assumption, Pareto also derived a theory of history wherein human history is seen as a circulation of elites.

Pareto comes to the conclusion that nonlogical actions form the greater part of man's social actions and, therefore, in formulating a theory to explain them, he will be able to understand the general form of society. Man's actions are seen by Pareto to originate from a constant element, the psychic state of the actor, which is made up of many sentiments, and of variable elements, the explanations, theories, and "pseudological" justifications of his actions. Moreover, Pareto concludes that the psychic states determining man's actions can be known only partially, through their manifestations and expressions in the actor's behavior.

The drama of Pareto the man, and the key to understanding his vision of an irrational, meaningless, and unchangeable world ruled by brute force and by cruelty—which are clearly portrayed in his work and Weltanschauung—is the drama of the "Seigneur humilié dans son sang," of the "Savant inécouté, mécompris, et rejetté dans sa science," and of the "Politicien défait et frustré dans ses ambitions"; most of all, however, it is the drama of the "idealiste desillusioné dans son ideal et incapable de le realiser," who witnesses the agonies and downfall of all he had idealized and striven for, the hopelessness of his most cherished ideals and ambitions. These crucial existential and psychological experiences slowly become the keynote of his entire psyche and of his total vision of man, society, and history.

During the second and vital part of his formative years, while he lived and worked in Florence, "Pareto began to feel in all its acuteness the suffering of his condition of humiliated scientist and nobleman. Humiliated to be unable to find the place to which he aspires, humiliated by the misery and decadence of the social class to which he belongs, humiliated to have to deal with people who ignore or scorn all the values which are the earmarks of his class."[9]

Likewise, during the last part of his formative period in Italy, when Pareto was knocking in vain at the doors of Italy's academias, he came to the conclusion, central to his entire thought and work, that reason and ideals were powerless and sterile; he saw them as an efflorescence of more primitive and powerful irrational forces.

At the turn of the century, when he finally abandoned Italy for an academic career in Switzerland, he universalized and projected his own personal experience onto the canvas of human societies and history. As his ideas and ideals, the flower of modern science and positivism, were powerless and could not affect the conduct of men and the destiny of his country, so were the ideas and ideals of other men powerless and sterile; it was not Pareto or Pareto's ideas which had failed, but the inexorable nature of things that had shown him the underlying reality of man, society, and history. And if we add his wife's actions to this, we can understand the psychological frame of mind of our "philosophe desabusé."

Pareto died at the age of seventy-five and lies buried in the small Celigny churchyard. "For a long time," Bousquet claims, "he seemed indifferent to almost everything; there is in him not the least bit of enthusiasm left for anything, for he no longer had any illusions about anything."[10] Pareto continued writing until his last day. Some of his later articles and essays were later assembled and published in two books: *Fatti e Teorie* (1920) and *Transformazione della Democrazia* (1921).

Pareto's Theory of Human Nature and His Conception of the Ideal Man

Unlike Comte and Durkheim, Pareto's aim was to separate rather than to integrate, to analyze rather than to synthesize, and to understand as much himself and his life as the world and the social system in which he lived. Instead of seeking to unite the head and the heart, he made it the cardinal premise of his system to keep them apart; instead of seeking to translate theory into practice and to realize ideals in reality, he advocated and practiced a complete divorce between them and treated all ideals, whether religious, political, or social, as the nonlogical and creative fabric of man's imagination. Instead of seeking to know and to understand man in order to improve and to perfect him, Pareto sought to know why he was what he was, to understand why he behaved the way he did, why the world treated him the way it did, and why he had failed in his practical endeavors in the second formative period of his life.

Pareto does not seek truth for the sake of action or to persuade and enlighten others. He states that the knowledge he seeks is inimical to man and to society; in revealing the roots and depths of man's animality, egoism, and irrationality, and in unveiling the true face and foundation of society—power, ruse, meaningless recurrence, and eternal exploitation of the weak by the strong—man is demoralized and disillusioned, and social integration is undermined. Hence, the "logico-experimental" knowledge of man and society should remain the property of the selected few.

Pareto came to conclusions similar to those of Marsilius de Padua, Machiavelli, Frazer, Le Bon, Sorel, Nietzsche, and Mosca. Superstitions, illusions, and nonlogical religious faiths are vital for the cohesion of human societies; rational investigations and scientific studies of man and society, in destroying the former, also undermine the integration of the personality system and of the social system. Thus he assumed the existential position and the intellectual perspective of a grand inquisitor. Scientific knowledge of man and of his social expressions is inimical to religion and, therefore, to the well-being of man and society. The higher development and liberation of humanity, therefore, is destined to remain a myth, a dangerous humanitarian fancy. The apparent advances of reason and of freedom, he assumed, would merely lead to ever new confrontations and struggles between a small number of elite at the expense of the masses, as they always have in the past.

From this, it is clear that Pareto did not embark on his quest for a scientific sociology for the sake of others. Likewise, it is equally clear that, under the name of pure science and of the quest for truth, be it heaven or hell, there stands Pareto himself and his need to rationalize and to justify to himself, if not to others, the course and events of his own life, the reasons for his failures and for his present predicament. Social and historical events are, to a large extent, peripheral to Pareto himself, being interpreted through the prism of his own Weltanschauung, which was formed in the economic and political arena of the Italy of the fin du siècle. He unwittingly universalized and projected his predicament onto the whole of human history.

Pareto's work, therefore, is far more than a sociological investigation into, and a treatise of, the social sciences; it is an intellectual autobiography, a philosophical and existential self-explanation and self-justification. The key to unlock Pareto's intellectual system and to penetrate into his mental universe, and to understand them in a broader perspective, lies, therefore, both in his personal life and in the sociocultural milieu in which he lived. Both provided the formative elements that fashioned his personality which, in turn, produced his work. At the very center of his intellectual system, moreover, lies his theory of human nature, his anthropology, which he explicitly made the cornerstone of his sociology and, in fact, of all social investigations.

Pareto's theory of human nature contains no genuine conception of an ideal man that might be generally realized; the archetype of all ideals, the ideal of man, does not exist and cannot exist. The centuries roll by and human nature remains the same, because man's will and ideas are powerless to transform him in his depths. Since the heart of man's being, described by Pareto's theory of the residues, is impenetrable, irrational, and constant, and since man's behavior is mostly nonlogical, meaningless, and ever recurrent, even though its verbal justifications and explanations are everchanging, and since man's will and reason are fallen and impotent, all ideals are illusions, self-deceptions, and epiphenomenal efflorescences of man's bio-psychic core, which lies forever beyond his reach.

The study of Pareto's theory of human nature proves by default my major hypothesis: a theory of human nature and of a conception of the ideal man, at the infrastructural and axiological foundation, is essential to social science. The study of Pareto's theory of human nature and the ideal man shows the presence and the significance of a *negative* conception of man and its profound consequences for a thinker's theoretical and methodological developments. It demonstrates, that is, that the conception of the ideal man is a formative and generative agent in the thought processes of its author, thus corroborating, from another angle, my basic assumption.

The essence of Pareto's vision of man, society, and history is rooted in materialism, unintelligibility, meaninglessness, egoism, power, and exploitation. Man, for him, is essentially an animal, but an animal with a fringe of rationality. Man has the desire for, and the illusion of, becoming something nobler and greater than he is. He is fully encompassed by nature and, therefore, by inexorable natural laws, a being without a higher nature and set of potentialities, a being without an evolution. Man cannot leave the world of nature for a sui generis world of society. His world is governed not so much by the social elite as by man's unchanging biopsychic residues with their fundamental core of irrationality. His life is a hell without a purpose, an existence without a direction and culmination, with no hope other than illusions and myths, or a disaffected and soul-corroding realism.

Pareto, although opposed to and rejecting the ideals of his time, was himself unable to fashion new ideals and ends for those he rejected; thus he ended up with skepticism, pessimism, and nihilism at the core of his philosophy. In the mature period of his life, he laughed at the "lame" instead of seeking to help them, because he no longer believed in, or hoped for, anything of true value. Toward the end of his career, in fact, Pareto degraded the only ideals he had preserved and worked for—science and rationality.

Pareto's theory of the derivations, although a valuable tool for penetrating through the veneer of ideologies, and propaganda, and for demythologizing man's social, political, and religious beliefs, never goes beyond a critical phase. It destroys and it demystifies, but it never constructs anything new in the place of what it has torn down. As St. Simon and Comte would have said: it never entered an "organic phase."

Nihilism and skepticism, which were the product of Pareto's crucial life experiences, are no adequate substitutes for simple beliefs and naive conceptions which, many times, embody deeper meanings and realities; Pareto's scorn and cynicism are not substitutes for the sympathy necessary to penetrate into and to understand the heart of man and the human dimension of society and history. Man cannot live amid intellectual, emotional, or physical ruins.

Pareto stopped at the end of his destructive sweep, exhausted and demoralized, never to build anew. For him, reason is fulfilled by linking logical means to rational ends. Domination and exploitation are natural phenomena, and all human societies are made up of two basic groups: a small minority of exploiters and oppressors and a large majority of exploited and oppressed. At the core of Pareto's universe and nihilistic vision of man and society is his conception of man as an irrational animal, who has a faint glow of rationality, self-knowledge, and self-mastery. In the penetrating words of Stark, Pareto was never a student of human sociality, of man's truly human nature; "he was merely an exponent of human nature—indeed, of man's lower nature—whose transformation by sociality he did not manage to understand."[11] What Pareto visualized and conceptualized was not man the social and human being, but man the biopsychic and presocial animal.

The theoretical and methodological center of Pareto's intellectual system is a theory of human nature—a theory of human cognition, a definition of man, and an aborted theory of eudaemonia and conception of the ideal man. In order to grasp both the axiological foundation of Pareto's thought and the theoretical implications of his sociological researches, it is necessary to first understand his conception of man.

The question, what is man? lies at the heart of Pareto's work. It stands behind his economic question—can a just distribution of wealth ever be achieved? It is also behind the political question he asked—how can the "best" be made to rule for the common good rather than for their selfish interests? And, it undergirds Pareto's major scientific question—can science bring progress and well-being to man at the social, moral, and human level, as well as at the material and technological level? What can man know, and how does he know? What is the true range of human behavior? What can man hope and strive for in his life? These are the fundamental questions he sought to answer and to articulate in his theory of human nature.

Pareto's theory of human nature can be found scattered throughout his work; but its essence and structural parts are in his theory of the residues and of the derivations. Its manifestation in human society and history is, however, in his theory of social heterogeneity and of the circulation of the elite. Briefly, the theoretical assumptions of Pareto's theory of human nature are the following:

1. Social phenomena are highly complex in their concrete historical manifestations, so they must be divided into two main classes: those involving logical and those involving nonlogical conduct. Nonlogical conduct is more prevalent and more important.
2. People have a tendency and a deep need to rationalize and "logicize" their behavior by means of theories that give their actions a semblance of rationality.
3. When examined in the light of the logico-experimental method, the various extant theories and rationalizations of human actions reveal both their nonlogical nature and their social and psychological usefulness in keeping the social system and the personality system integrated. This discovery led Pareto to postulate that experimental truth and social utility are functionally antithetical to each other.
4. The analysis of social facts, that is, of social, political, and philosophical theories, by the logico-experimental method reveals, moreover, that man's actions and theories contain two basic sets of elements. First, the nonlogical elements are the true mainspring of human behavior and remain essentially constant; second, the pseudo-rational elements are rationalizations and justifications of the highly variable nonlogical side of human nature. Thus he explicitly told Pantaleoni: "The theories and beliefs of men are but the clothes of the sentiments which alone are the efficient motors of human actions."[12]

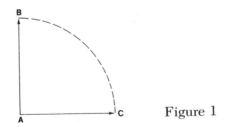

Figure 1

With these basic assumptions and conclusions, Pareto laid the groundwork for his theory of human nature. It is succinctly represented by Figure 1. A represents the constant and causal elements Pareto called the "residues"; B represents their theoretical "logicization" and explanation, what Pareto called the "derivations"; and C represents human actions, what Pareto called the "derivatives." Thus, in the *Trattato*, Pareto writes:

Let us make the elements A and B our main concern. The element A corresponds, we may guess, to certain instincts of man, or more exactly *men*, because A has no objective existence and differs in different individuals; and it is probably because of its correspondence to certain instincts that it is virtually constant in social phenomena. The element B represents the work of the mind in accounting for A. That is why B is much more variable, as reflecting the play of the imagination. But if the element A corresponds to certain instincts, it is far from reflecting them all.[13]

Pareto was careful, however, not to fully identify his residues with the sentiments or instincts to which they correspond and which they express in overt behavior.

The residues A must not be confused with the sentiments or instincts to which they correspond. The residues are the manifestations of sentiments and instincts just as the rising of the mercury is a manifestation of the rise in temperature. . . . The completed statements would be: the sentiments or instincts that correspond to residues, along with those corresponding to appetites, interests, etc., are the main factors in determining the social equilibrium.[14]

Pareto formulated a classification, or typology, of the residues, which represent the constant, causal, unintelligible, and irrational drives behind men's actions. This classification forms the core of his theory of human nature.[15]

Class 1: Instinct for combinations. This class deals with the desire and need to coordinate heterogeneous elements into new compositions, to meaningfully synthesize the manifold parts of human experience. This class of residues, according to Pareto, has been a primary factor behind all intellectual syntheses and systems of thought. And, as such, it is the driving element behind the growth of social classes and of civilization in general.

Class 2: Persistence of aggregates. This class deals with the desire and need for preserving in existence what has been realized, either materially or intellectually. This second class is the polar opposite of the first. The first corresponds to the need for innovation and change, and the second corresponds to the need for conservation and order.

Class 3: Need for expressing sentiments by external acts. This class deals with the desire and need to express emotions and sentiments by overt acts.

Class 4: Residues connected with sociality. Pareto sees social life as resulting from certain residues, much as William McDougall in his instinctivistic theory or John Watson in his behavioristic theory. Men, he postulates, have an instinctive need for each other and thus for social groups.

Class 5: Integrity of the individual and his appurtenances. Just as there is a set of instincts and sentiments which lead to the formation of groups and self-discipline (the price of living in a group), so there are opposite instincts and sentiments that lead to fighting for well-being and self-preservation, for self-interest and self-integrity. Just as there are forces that tend to reestablish the social equilibrium when the latter is upset, so there are forces that tend to preserve and to restore the equilibrium of the psyche, and these forces Pareto calls the "residues of the integrity of the individual and his appurtenances."

Class 6: The sex residue. For Pareto sex plays a fundamental role in human affairs, but he did not classify as residues the instinctive drive for *direct* sexual expression. Rather he looked at the sexual drive through its influence on man's way of thinking and the explanations man formulates to account for his behavior.

Pareto's theory of the residues is an attempt to plunge into the depths of man to conceptualize the constant and more substantial part of his being—the animal, irrational, and unintelligible part. As Borkenau summarized it, Pareto's residues have two basic traits:

> They represent the common underlying psychological element in different actions. They are invariable and they are incapable of any further explanation. Social life is determined by a considerable number of these unchangeable and uncommutable psychological entities which, themselves, have neither a function nor a meaning nor even an origin: they are simply there. Or rather, it is not society which, in the first place, is determined by these residues but the life of the individual, no social element entering into the concept of residue itself. Pareto's sociology is individualistic in the extreme, abstracting entirely as it does from the very necessities of social cooperation.[16]

Pareto's complete theory of human nature, however, also considers man's desperate attempts to hide the essence of his being under a cloak of reason and intelligibility. The theory of derivations is Pareto's attempt to account, in part, for the flickering of human rationality and for the effort to rationalize instinctive behavior. Derivations account subjectively for the production of thought systems, rationalizations, and justifications of man's irrational behavior; the residues account objectively for them. Derivations thus constitute the theories and reasons that men of all times have given to explain their behavior, which is, in the final analysis, the product of the residues. Pareto explains: "Residues are very hard to modify. Derivations are stretched to any length required, like rubber bands."[17] And, "derivations are effective only when they are in harmony with residues which are the real motors behind human conduct."[18]

Pareto formulates a classification, or typology, of the derivations:[19]

Class 1. Assertion. These include assertion of fact, of sentiment, and of both fact and sentiment. This class deals with dogmatic statements which simply claim that x is x without offering any proof for their assertions.

Class 2: Authority. Appeal is made to some kind of authority as proof of the veracity of a claim in order to increase its convincing power.

Class 3: Accord with sentiments or principles. These derivations are related to the residues of sociality. Accord with sentiments or conceptions of public opinion or of experts lends great persuasive force to these derivations, regardless of the logicoexperimental truth.

Class 4: Verbal proofs. This class of derivations deals with the pseudologic which is anchored in vague and ambiguous terms rather than in experimental proof.

Elucidating the key implications of his theory of residues and derivations, Pareto writes:

> Given certain residues and certain derivations, two sorts of problems arise: 1. Just how do such residues and derivations function? 2. What is the bearing of their action on social utility? Ordinary empiricism deals with two problems at once, either failing to distinguish them or distinguishing them inadequately. A scientific analysis has to keep them distinct; and it is essential, if one is to avoid falling into ready error, that while one is dealing with the first, one's mind should not be encumbered with the second.[20]

Such is Pareto's analytical and structural theory of human nature; its functional and practical application can be found in his theory of social heterogeneity and of the circulation of the elite, and, for that matter, in his theory of social equilibrium and throughout his entire work. Its influence permeated all his theoretical and methodological developments. S. E. Finer evaluates Pareto's contributions to modern social thought:

> He is the first sociologist to recognize that a complete science of social relations must include the personality system as well as the

multiplex factors of the social system, and correspondingly to make his theory of personality an overt and integral part of his system. We showed, indeed, that one principal reason for the inadequacy of his whole system was precisely the inadequacy of his theory of personality; but this emphasizes how central a part it plays.[21]

Human nature is complex, and the term can mean many things to different people; moreover, it is not a homogeneous whole but, rather, a heterogeneous juxtaposition of qualitatively different elements. The Greek thinkers, for example, used to view man as a threefold being made up of a physical part, or "soma," man's biological organism; of a psychosocial part, or "psyche," man's psychosocial personality; and of a spiritual part or "pneuma," man's divine spirit. Likewise, the idealistic and mystical traditions claimed that in each person sleeps a beast, a man, and a god, and according to how a person lives and thinks, so will he awake and develop either his animal, his human, or his spiritual nature. The Greeks embodied this fundamental insight graphically in the great symbol of the Sphinx with its animal body (instincts and passions), its human head (reason and will), and its eaglelike wings (the potentialities of spiritual intuition and inspiration).

Modern thought since the Enlightenment, particularly the social sciences, has come to recognize and to investigate man's physical nature and animal tendencies, and man's psychosocial nature and human tendencies, neglecting for the most part, or collapsing into the psychosocial, man's spiritual nature and potentialities.

Pareto, I contend, concentrates on only a third of human reality, and, furthermore, the part he does focus on, man's biopsychic nature, is the least important and the least "human." Pareto's theory of human nature is a series of philosophical and metaphysical speculations on man's prerational, presocial, and prehuman nature, of that part which man shares with the animal kingdom and not of the distinctly social and human part. Thus Pareto sees human nature as remaining essentially constant and unaffected in its depths by sociocultural changes.

The animals, being driven by instincts, have a constant set of drives, which do not change. Their social behavior, as in the case of the hymenoptera, does not change throughout the centuries; bees and ants as well as horses and chimpanzees always behave in the same fashion generation after generation; they have no history, no true culture, and no unfoldment of consciousness or higher faculties—the particular and distinctive privilege that makes man truly human.

In conclusion, for Pareto man is a biopsychic animal characterized by biopsychic drives, by an ineluctable and unchanging egoism, and by a mere fringe of rationality and will.

Pareto's second fundamental theoretical development, after his theory of the residues and of the derivations, is his theory of the circulation of the elite, which undergirds the equilibrium of the social system and the cycles of history. This theory is rooted in four basic assumptions and conclusions concerning what man is and represents the theory's projection on the social stage. First, man is a purely natural being, fully encompassed by laws of nature he can never transcend. Second, natural and inexorable inequality in basic physical, intellectual, and moral endowments on all levels is the unchangeable and permanent lot of men. Third, domination and exploitation of the masses by a small and well-organized elite is a natural and, therefore, an inescapable phenomenon. The distribution of the residues in man's biopsychic make-up brings out the two key classes of society: the elite, subdivided into the ruling and the nonruling elite; and the ruled masses. Fourth, there is always a certain degree of class antagonism between the rulers and the ruled, which is due to their different personality structures and intellectual perspectives. Thus, governing entails both a struggle to gain power and a struggle to retain power.

In the ruling elite and the nonruling elite, two kinds of men emerge; each has a different distribution and predominance of residues. These Pareto calls the "lions" and the "foxes." The lions, who have a prevalence of class 2 and class 4 residues, tend to rule through "force" and "faith," while the foxes, who have a prevalence of class 1 and class 5 residues, tend to rule through "cunning" and "fraud." The circulation of the elite is, therefore, an alternation of lions and foxes in the ruling positions of society. This alternation follows more or less the following cycle: a ruling elite that is unwilling or unable to maintain its privileged position by the use of force, easily falls prey to another elite that is willing and able to do so. The first elite of foxes is thus replaced by a new elite of lions.

The political phase of this cycle is followed closely by an economic phase where "speculators," men rich in class 1 residues, correspond to the foxes, and "rentiers," men rich in class 2 residues, correspond to the lions.

For Pareto, moreover, it is the clash between the speculators and the rentiers, the foxes and the lions, and not that between the capitalists and the workers, which constitutes the fundamental source of conflict in human societies that, in turn, determines the cycle of history.

Finally, the political and economic cycles are likewise correlated with an intellectual-cultural cycle that pits "men of skepticism and science" against "men of faith and religion." In each case, there is a conflict and a struggle between two fundamental types of men, those in whom class 1 residues predominate and those in whom class 2 residues predominate. Social dynamics and historical developments end up being the projection and the working out of biopsychic residues. Society and history, therefore, appear as the creations of the irrational, unintelligible, and changeless residues, which vary in distribution and intensity but not in essence.

Underlying and animating the thought and the life of Pareto, I found as I did for that of Comte and Durkheim, but with different premises and conclusions, two fundamental quests: a quest for knowledge and a quest for self-realization. The first quest ended in an articulation of a theory of human nature. By studying man's works and expressions in society through history, this quest became the foundation of Pareto's entire intellectual edifice. This theory consisted of two basic parts: a conception of man and a theory of human cognition. The second quest led him to seek self-realization and self-fulfillment in commercial and industrial ventures and in the realization of economic and political ideas. These failed miserably; Pareto became profoundly disillusioned and abandoned all practical activities and all hope to realize himself in the affairs of the world. Henceforth, he dedicated his intelligence and energies to an understanding and explanation, to himself if not to others, of why he had failed to realize concretely his ideals and theories.

From what man does, writes, and says, Pareto worked his way down into the depths of man's psyche and sought to uncover and to classify that which drives human behavior. Underpinning all Pareto's social and historical manifestations of the human psyche and its life springs, stands his theory of human cognition, which structures his theory of human action. His sociological and historical studies are two main avenues by which he seeks to formulate a consistent theory of human nature; and his anthropology as a whole constitutes the axiological foundation upon which his sociological and historical analyses rest. These two, therefore, stand in dialectical relationship to each other, proceeding from the outward, objective actions and expressions to the inward, subjective states of consciousness via the inductive method and then back from the inward, subjective consciousness, to the outward, objective actions, via the deductive method.

Pareto never truly investigated or formulated his theory of human cognition; he merely transposed it, uncritically, from his earlier studies in mathematics and physics to the study of economic and, later, of social phenomena. As Talcott Parsons tersely put it: "Pareto's explicit methodology was derived mainly from his experience in the physical sciences."[22]

Pareto merely borrowed uncritically his theory of human cognition from one of the central currents of the Zeitgeist of his time and, later, reaffirmed it through his own personal experiences as an engineer and as an economist. Pareto's theory of human cognition rests on two premises. First, valid scientific knowledge can only be derived from observational data that are classified and interpreted by human reason following the strict canons of logic; valid scientific knowledge is "logico-experimental" knowledge. Second, all reality is one, uniform, continuous, and homogeneous, without qualitative jumps; there are no heterogeneous breaks or discontinuities, no qualitatively different planes or dimensions merging into each other at the experiential level. In short, reality and truth are unidimensional and flat.

From these two central premises, Pareto deduced, without much critical thinking, that the model by which to represent conceptually all reality is that of *rational mechanics*. Consequently, the concepts and postulates of rational mechanics, which he studied in school and which he applied as an engineer, became the paradigms for all scientific knowledge, whether concerned with inanimate or animate realms. Later in his life, he used this model to analyze the actions of human beings in the social system. Thus, in the *Trattato*, he writes:

> Let us consider the molecules of the social system; in other words, individuals who are possessed of certain sentiments manifested by residues—which, for the sake of brevity, we shall designate simply as residues. We may say that present in individuals are mixtures of groups of residues that are analogues to the mixtures of chemical compounds found in nature, the group of residues themselves being analogous to the chemical compounds.[23]

This paradigm of rational mechanics, applied indiscriminately to all phenomena, constitutes the central methodological bias of Pareto and is one of his basic errors. By the inappropriate utilization of this model, human realities are stripped of their sui generis qualities and are reduced to the dynamics of lifeless systems. This model also, therefore, denatured Pareto's fundamental assumptions about human nature and his central conclusions regarding the dynamics, the coherence, and change of the social system.

When investigating economic phenomena, Pareto already realized that a large part of human behavior did not fit easily into this mode; human and social reality is far too complex and intricate to be explained rationally. The social phenomena that could not fit into this model, he classified, a priori, as nonlogical, that is, as ultimately unintelligible and unexplainable, as instinct and sentiment-driven.

At the theoretical and methodological level, Pareto's uncritical theory of human cognition led him to the fundamental distinction between logical and nonlogical actions, between the subjective view of the actor and the objective view of the scientific observer, and between reason-directed and sentiment-driven behavior. This arbitrary distinction, moreover, was further reinforced and concretized, at the experiential and psychological levels, by Pareto's political experiences and idealistic disillusionments.

At the beginning of his studies and until Pareto renounced the world of action for the world of contemplation, it is possible to see the embryonic roots of an ideal man springing forth and undergirding his Mazzinist-liberal ideals. At that point in Pareto's life, the good man must have appeared to him as the man of science, who seeks knowledge of himself, of his society and its history in order to improve himself and to contribute to the growth of his nation on all levels—intellectual, scientific, technological, economic, social, and political.

The good person would receive a solid training in mathematics and the natural sciences and would internalize the paradigmatic model of rational mechanics, which he would now apply to the study of man and social phenomena. The good person would develop a rational theory of economics and political science and would use his conclusions to improve the life of man; he would develop a "scientific sociology," which would pave the way to the reorganization of European society, bringing in its wake greater economic prosperity, greater equality and freedom of expression for all, and less exploitation, misery, and violence of man to man. The good person would know himself and his society so that he could realize himself to the fullest extent and lead others to do likewise. This person would use rational arguments rather than force to gain his maximum good, which was also the common good.

Once Pareto had been defeated in his practical economic and political endeavors, abandoned by his wife, had come to the realization that most of human behavior is irrational and sentiment-driven, and that ideas and ideals are powerless to influence social events and to improve human nature, the picture changes. As optimism turns to pessimism, and he becomes more and more disillusioned, Pareto's ideals begin to dim, bringing in their wake an eclipse of the greatest of all of man's ideals—the ideal of man himself.

Human nature is fundamentally unfathomable and unintelligible, hence reasons and ideals are a frail efflorescence of deeper instinctive forces, and man is an egoistical and power-hungry beast who will ever remain such. With these basic assumptions and conclusions, a true conception and realization of an ideal man, or of the good man of tomorrow, is not possible. Nevertheless, in his mature years, and at the center of Pareto's intellectual synthesis, are indications leading to a conception of what man should be once he is "illuminated" by the conclusions of Pareto's sociology and by a logico-experimental study of human nature and of the nature of society and history. This superior man, which Pareto sought to become and to articulate, stands behind his *Trattato*, his courses on sociology, and his major mature teachings.

Two major assumptions underlie this conception. First, although reason and science cannot change or improve human nature and the sociohistorical processes that depend on human nature, they can show why things happen the way they do. The role of reason and of scientific understanding here is purely illuminative and no longer active or creative. Second, science should, by its nature and psychosocial consequences, remain the privilege of a small minority; it cannot and should not be popularized and spread to the masses, because the masses would then be demoralized and the social system would lose some of its indispensable cohesion.

The best that can be done is to become a sociologist in Pareto's sense. The quest for self-realization and its theoretical formulation, the theory of eudaemonia, are to be discarded as unrealizable owing to the nature of man; only the quest for truth, the quest for a logico-experimental knowledge of human nature and of the dynamics of society, are to be retained.

The good man here, the sociologist, is a sardonic grand inquisitor who dares to look human and social reality in the face. This person will be completely honest and frank with himself; he will assiduously cultivate the model of rational mechanics, which is the highest model for objective thinking, and turn it towards the riddle of the sphinx, the investigation of human nature and of its outward expressions in human societies. This person will endeavor to penetrate through all the layers of derivations, ideologies, and ideals to the bedrock of human nature and to the foundations of the social order. He will dare to see man as he really is in his animal nature and society as it really functions in all its inhumanity. Childish illusions about the goodness and the purpose of human life will be given up for the sake of knowledge and understanding; the human exploitation and social inequality underlying all social existence will be uncovered.

It is the man who sees man as he is: an egoistical, irrational, and purposeless animal without a destiny, an animal driven by his residues which spin out countless derivations, "ideals," and theories to deceive himself and others, to assuage his anxiety and loneliness, and to make his life psychosocially more bearable. It is the man who will accept himself as he is without seeking to be anything else or hoping to become a better man. It is the man who sees life only in terms of personal survival, of biopsychic adaptation and psychosocial adjustment; the man who strives to gain the most power and freedom for himself without giving any thought to unfolding himself or to actualizing a higher being in himself; a man for whom the true purpose and meaning of life—the realization of ideals and the fashioning of a greater and fuller self—has been lost and who, therefore, seeks to while life away in the most pleasant and comfortable way possible.

It is the man who will express his residues as fully as possible without much regard for others; the man who will not refrain from using cunning and force, *astuzia* and *crudelta*, to obtain his ends and to maintain his privileged position; it is the man who, being "enlightened" about his own nature and drives, will use his knowledge of instinctual dynamics to work upon the feelings and sentiments of others to achieve his ends. In short, it is the thoroughly realistic and disenchanted man who sees man at his lowest common denominator, his selfish and animal nature, and who will treat him, and himself, as such.

Pareto's superior person clearly differentiates between reason and sentiment; sentiment is the greatest enemy of science, and of sociology in particular. Thus Pareto wrote to Pantaleoni: "With all my strength, I seek to be immune from hatred and from love; I have renounced all propaganda activities to defend or to attack any cause whatever and to seek to affect events: I observe them and that is all."[24]

The superior person in Pareto's universe clearly stands outside the social system and has withdrawn from the battle of life in order to investigate them scientifically and to evaluate them objectively. It is clearly Pareto himself. Thus he acknowledged that his own intellectual system is the product of his social isolation. Accordingly, he told Pantaleoni: "It is certain that [my sociology] is the fruit of the special conditions of my life and that it was and is for me a singular fortune to be able to live at Celigny away from the noise of the world."[25]

The intellectual aim is to discover the true mainsprings of the countless verbal explanations, justifications, and speculations, particularly in the political, economic, and religious fields. This is the aim Pareto set for himself and for the small elite of future sociologists. "I want to take off the halo by which the stupid public has crowned all the humanitarian saints and show them as they are in reality."[26]

Pareto, in terms of his own schema, strove to balance class 1 and class 2 residues; he tried to cultivate dispassionate scientific knowledge and a realistic awareness of human nature and of the dynamics of the social system; he tried to dismiss illusions and idealistic notions. If he were to participate in human affairs, in social life and in political action in particular, he would then know how to use the sentiments, the ideals, and the superstitions of others for his own interest. He would, above all, be willing to use force whenever necessary to keep men in line—the human animal understands and is affected far more by force than he is by the arguments and demonstrations of reason. This he made quite clear in his writings and letters. "Had Louis XVI not been a man of little sense and less courage, letting himself be floored without fighting and preferring to lose his head on the guillotine to dying weapon in hand like a man of sinew, he might have been the one to do the destroying."[27] And, "The majority of men is composed of imbeciles and of a few rascals; thus force is necessary to restrain them; and in the periods of transition, when this is impossible, all one can do is to laugh at the imbeciles and at the rascals."[28]

Pareto's Theory of Human Nature and Conception of the Ideal Man in His Life and Intellectual System

Pareto's ideal of the superior man, which is clearly derived from his conception of human nature and from his crucial life experiences, is, in a sense, a fusion in one man of some of the characteristics of the fox, the lion, the speculator, the rentier, the man of skepticism, and the man of faith—all creatures of his own intellectual system. This ideal is well portrayed by a statement he made in one of his letters to Pantaleoni: "One must have an iron hand in a glove of velvet."[29]

Pareto's aim seems to have been to combine toughmindedness, the realism and the scientific precision of the man with a preponderance of class 1 residues, with the commitment to principle and the willingness to use force of the man with a preponderance of class 2 residues; to combine some of the social instincts of class 4 with the clearly-realized and deliberately sought interests for self-integrity and self-preservation of class 5 residues; and finally to combine the need to express one's sexuality freely without self-deception or guilt with social life. In short, the superior person tries to be vital, healthy, and clever, seeking above all self-preservation and self-expression. The superior man, knowing himself, the residues of human nature, and the dynamics of the social system, will live by the laws of the "master-morality."

Motivating all Pareto's investigations, economic, political, and sociological, is the Delphic injunction, know thyself. Pareto, the extreme nominalist, sees the individual at the core of society and, therefore, of any sociology. In consequence, man and a scientific knowledge of his nature and expressions are the theoretical foundation of both Pareto's intellectual system and the set of assumptions in which all investigations in the social sciences must be rooted. The theoretical, psychological, and existential interplay between Pareto's theory of human nature and his intellectual system, and, the interplay between Pareto's thought and his life in the perspective of his sociocultural milieu are now clear.

From his family's background, Pareto derived the Mazzinist liberal and democratic views and ideals of the first part of his life. From his crucial life experiences as an engineer and a businessman, as an economist and an amateur politician in the turbulent and corrupt climate of the Italy of the fin du siècle, and as a betrayed and abandoned husband, he derived his distinction between reason and emotions, between behavior directed by reason and behavior driven by sentiment, and his distinction between the scientific truth of a theory and its social utility.

At the practical and existential levels, therefore, it was his quest for self-realization that aborted; his failure to realize and implement his most cherished ideals reinforced the fundamental distinction of his intellectual system between logical and nonlogical actions. At the psychological and temperamental level, moreover, Pareto poured forth all the highly passionate and idealistic strivings of his soul into this practical failure with two basic consequences: First, he tried to universalize and to project onto the history of the world his own personal political experiences and struggles. Second, his former optimism, love for humanity, and desire to realize himself through an active and constructive participation in the affairs of life turned into a growing pessimism, into contempt and detachment, and into a complete divorce between his quest for truth and his quest for self-realization.

The existential vicissitudes of Pareto's own life led him to postulate that most people and most human actions are driven by irrational sentiments and instincts, which follow a logic of their own. During his second formative period, he gave up all practical and active intervention in the affairs of life to dedicate himself to pure research and teaching; the theoretical and practical strands of his thought converged and crystallized in his final theory of human nature. At this point, he also began to see reason as powerless in relation to the residues, and he severed the two main strivings of his life, abandoning his theory of eudaemonia, and dedicated himself solely to an explanation of social structures and human actions—mainly to account for his own life experiences and failures. At this point, finally, the fundamental insights and premises of his mature intellectual synthesis emerged:

1. Ideas and ideals are not influences that can transform human nature and the social system, but variable epiphenomena of the residues.
2. Human nature remains fundamentally the same—irrational, unintelligible, and unchangeable.
3. Man and his collective expressions in society and history are purely natural phenomena, fully encompassed and determined by nature with no unfoldment of higher possibilities.
4. Truth, at least in the human and social spheres, is antithetical to human well-being and to social integration. Hence, it should not be disseminated through the masses; in any case, few men would ever be able to realize it.
5. Man is basically a biological entity and an instinctive animal with no higher nature or potentialities; hence, he is eternally destined to remain an egocentric and selfish being, and society and human affairs are ruled by force and cunning which should be used to personal advantage.

When Pareto saw the irrationality of the human psyche, he despaired of ever utilizing a knowledge of human nature to improve man and society. He renounced, both theoretically and practically, a conception of the ideal man. If there is no emergence of higher traits, no realization of ideals, there can be no genuine conception of, or strivings toward, an ideal man.

So long as Pareto believed in progress and did not explicitly formulate his theory of human nature, he had a latent conception of an ideal man; and so long as he had even a covert notion of an ideal man and a dim hope of unfolding the higher potentialities of human nature, he participated fully in the affairs of life.

Pareto renounced an active life for a contemplative one, because both theoretically, experientially, and psychologically he had given up his conception of an ideal man to realize in his person and in his life. At this point Pareto renounces practice for theory, action for reflection, and human strivings for "sardonic laughter"; he exchanges optimism for pessimism, faith for skepticism, and ideals for criticisms. His implicit conception of an unfoldment for man, of a good or ideal man, pales and vanishes. His final and mature theory of human nature is finally concretized and formalized. Behind his abandonment of action and participation in life lies a concept of the ideal man and its vicissitudes. This concept and insight cannot be underestimated; it is a kingpin of his theory of human nature, and it underlies all his theoretical and methodological developments. It had a farreaching effect on his personal life and on the growth and crystallization of his entire sociological synthesis.

Realizing that the naive rationalism and idealism that had issued from the intellectual revolutions of the Renaissance and the Enlightenment had failed to produce the long-expected and much-desired results, Pareto, with many of his contemporaries, plunged into an exploration of man's psychic depths, hoping to find the key to man's being and future. But, instead of turning toward man's spiritual nature and superconscious, Pareto and many others turned toward man's animal nature and unconscious; for these thinkers man lacks an ideal by which to seek self-realization.

5

MAX WEBER

The Man, His Work, and His Sociocultural Milieu

Max Weber, one of those geniuses who rarely appear in this world, grew up in the nineteenth century and flourished in our own time. His powerful, tormented, and penetrating soul was fashioned by the cultural traditions and the intellectual currents of Germany's First Reich; he reached his creative maturity in the Second Reich, which heard but did not heed the warnings of his work, and it prefigured the later emergence of the Third Reich. But Max Weber, who was proclaimed the greatest German academician, sociologist, and, perhaps, even politician of this century, was not only a genius and a great social scientist, he was also the prophet of the modern industrial world, the muffled and suffering conscience of Germany, and one of the most brilliant incarnations of European reason.

As a result of Weber's struggles, the soul of Germany and the spirit of the twentieth century found a voice. Weber's was the voice of reason, the voice of faith in humanity, and the voice of courage and steadfastness before the onslaught of unleashed irrational forces. In his creative genius flowed the internal stresses of his titanic nature, the vicissitudes of his family's saga, and the formative experiences of his own biography, as well as the problems and the paradoxes of his time. Through his consciousness, through his pen and his voice, these myriad antagonistic elements found clear expression and objectification; through the synthetic and creative power of Weber's mind, they culminated in a Promethean effort which laid the methodological and theoretical foundations of modern social science.

In Weber, man found new levels of expression and the ruthless objectivity to face life in the modern world without illusions. Finally, in his own life, the metaphysical malaise of the nineteenth century, the "maladie de la fin du siècle," found expression. The old and the new world, the Enlightenment and its romantic reaction, freedom and bureaucratization, charisma and reason, clashed, fused, and found an articulate synthesis.

Most of Weber's biographers, students, and critics concur that the mystery of his personality and creative genius, and the key to fathom his vision of the world, can only be understood within the twin perspectives of his personal life and of the sociocultural milieu in which he lived, both of which were projected, rationalized, and objectified in his work. Arthur Mitzman explains:

> Max Weber's shadow falls long over the intellectual life of our era. . . . At the heart of Weber's vision lies only the truth of his epoch, his country, and his station, the truth of a Bourgeois scholar in Imperial Germany. It was developed under agonizing personal pressures, themselves exerted and maintained by the dilemmas of family, social milieu, and historical position. The broadest ramifications of these dilemmas . . . are the dilemmas of a man of passion in a highly repressive family situation and society which, in parallel ways and under the threats of madness and social ostracism, blocked the expression of passion.[1]

Max Weber, as man endowed with an extraordinary sensitivity as well as with an enormous curiosity and a penetrating intellect, was driven by the desire to understand the meaning of his own existence, to understand the meaning of human existence in general, and to comprehend the causal forces and motives that stood behind and structured human action. As a result, he meditated at length on the significance of the influences that shaped his personal biography and he observed keenly and reflected on the significance of the major historical and contemporary events of his society and their consequences for the destiny of Germany. Better than most people, he realized that his own personality, Weltanschauung, and creative strivings were largely the product of sociocultural and biopsychic forces; his intellectual system and sociopolitical philosophy were the result of these forces reflected and rationalized by his unique creative genius.

Max Weber was a man of contradictions; his creative and restless genius manifested itself precisely by looking the existential and personal dichotomies squarely in the face and by fashioning a rational synthesis of them at the philosophical level. This intensification and rationalization of the eternal dualities and antinomies of human life, and his prolonged and heroic battles with himself and with the irrational and coercive forces he found in his social milieu made Max Weber the universal genius he was. Karl Jaspers keenly sensed this existential root in Weber's mind and work.

> Max Weber was a contradictory personality. On the one hand, the commanding figure with his grand gestures and bewitching eloquence. On the other, the anonymity of his almost obscure existence. On the one hand, the grace of his movements, his warmth of heart, the child-like simplicity of his purely human interests—on the other, the stern, uncompromising seeker after truth, which at times so overpowered him as to make him curse God.

Weber had a deep passion for knowledge, but he was indifferent to all his achievements. He seemed fully dedicated to the philosophy and methodology of science while also looking for the "authentic truth of Being." He had an "unswerving devotion" to strict methodology while holding that "all knowledge is relative." He could just as easily break with people whose principles disappointed him as he could show kindness and forgiveness. He combined a great serenity and capacity for joy with a "deep and searing anger." He could be uncompromising with the ethical imperatives of his nation while having a "lucid awareness of the demons of the night."[2]

Weber's existential and cognitive orientation, like his personality, contains fundamental dichotomies, which his tormented genius sought to reconcile in a grand synthesis. Foremost among these is his quandary in choosing between the active life of the politician and the contemplative life of the scholar and scientist. His first passion was the quest for truth—the detached study of philosophy and the sciences; he tried to grasp the meaning of human existence and the significance of his actions, as well as of other men's actions, in his society. His later yearning and overwhelming desire was the quest for self-realization and the material, intellectual, moral, and political elevation of the German people—the committed and partisan life of the politician.

In his life, however, Max Weber succeeded in fully developing only his quest to become a scholar and a scientist. His quest to become a politician and a statesman remained, because of his health, mainly at an embryonic stage and was finally expressed in his speeches and writings.

Max Weber, who under his highly developed self-restraint, rationality, and scientific objectivity, was an emotional volcano of seething conflicts and passion, beautifully embodied Pascal's famous insight:

"Man is internally torn by a war between his reason and his passions. Were there but reason without passions. . . . Were there but passions without reason. . . . But since both exist, man is in a perpetual state of inner strife since peace with one side of his nature signifies war with the other. Thus man is eternally divided against himself."[3] This struggle lasted throughout Weber's life with an unequivocal victory of reason over passion, with a reification of both in the philosophical struggle between science and religion into the opposites rationality and charisma.

Then followed the moral dilemma of choosing between an "ethic of success" *(Erfolgsethik)* and an "ethic of responsibility" *(Gesinnungsethik);* between the moral principles of Machiavelli and Bismarck and those of Jesus and Tolstoy. The ultimate reconciliation and synthesis, at least at the existential level, came by assigning the two ethics to different types of men and to different levels in man. The ethic of responsibility belongs to the politician and the statesman, which Weber adopted in his public life, and the ethic of ultimate values belongs to the saint and the hero, which he adopted in his private life.

Finally, antinomies emerged between asceticism and eudaemonism, stoicism and pessimism, and faith and despair. Weber oscillated most of his life between these antinomies and finally resolved them by combining them through a delicate psychic balance and a vision of the world best characterized as a "heroic stoicism" and "enlightened pessimism."

The existential roots of these profound antinomies, interwoven dialectically both in his life and in his intellectual system, can be traced to two influences: his family background and his own nature; both were immersed in the issues and tensions of the society in which he lived. These antinomies, moreover, were further reinforced and objectified by his precarious physical and emotional health, which prevented him from realizing his ideals and self as he ardently desired.

Like his contemporary fellow sociologists, Weber was a grand-child of the Enlightenment and was deeply influenced by its intellectual, social, and political revolutions—both in what he accepted and incorporated from them, and in what he reacted against and rejected as a "philosopher's dream." Like his fellow sociologists, he incorporated in his own thinking and works, the romantic reaction to the Enlightenment and the progressive disenchantment with its great ideals and magnificent promises without, however, being able to disown them completely.

The Enlightenment and the French Revolution, industrialization and urbanization, in ushering in the modern world had failed to bring about the "Kingdom of God on earth": freedom, equality, brother-hood, and a greater actualization of human potentialities; rather, they had brought about an everincreasing rationalization, a disenchant-ment with the world and with life, a new form of exploitation and a new form of slavery for the masses. This time slavery was caused not so much by other men as by the flower of man's genius and creative ability: science and bureaucracy.

Max Weber was born on 21 April 1864, in Erfurt, Thuringia, and died in 1920. His life, therefore, spanned and witnessed the birth of the German nation, its victory at Sedan, unification under Bismarck, and its defeat and humiliation in 1918. Like many German scholars of his generation, Weber was born into an upper-middle class with considerable wealth, political influence, and social contacts. His fa-ther was a successful lawyer and a figure in Germany's local and national politics. Leading intellectuals and politicians frequently vis-ited the Webers and brought a cultivated and cosmopolitan intellec-tual atmosphere into their house. Through the early conditioning of this social milieu, Weber came in contact with the major realities and problems of his society.

Weber grew up in a German nation that had recently been unified, but which had been left without any outstanding political leadership after the dismissal of Bismarck. "The new Germany was a political cauldron with strong Left, Center, and Right movements surrounding a power-oriented monarchy."[4]

During Weber's lifetime three major developments took place in Germany. First, from a series of kingdoms, duchies, and principalities, Germany was unified into a modern nation. Second, industrialization and urbanization developed at a rapid rate and created profound sociocultural changes and dislocations. Third, imperialism and Euro-pean military and political supremacy—the quest for overseas col-onies, a rising interdependence with European nations, and the use of military force to achieve political objectives—these became an official state policy.

These three major developments converged in Germany, which had a weak civil leader in Kaiser Wilhelm II as well as many highly complex social, political, and economic problems. In Germany, philosophers and social scientists had become deeply concerned with the decline of traditionalism and the shift from the small face-to-face community, to the large, impersonal city, and with the passage from an aristocratic-feudal society to a democratic-capitalistic one. Thus in the Germany of Weber's time the old and the new, the "high" and the "low," authoritarianism and freedom stood side by side generating enormous tensions, contradictions, and dislocations.

While France had evolved toward an essentially positivistic philosophical position, which integrated empiricism and rationalism, Germany had crystallized around an idealistic philosophical position. The key assumption of the German idealistic tradition of social thought can be briefly summarized in the following words: Between the phenomenal and the spiritual world, and between the world of the natural sciences and the world of the social sciences, there exists an unsurmountable chasm—human consciousness.

One of the great problems that this epistemological and philosophical position raised was that of establishing how to arrive at a valid understanding of human behavior. As the monistic position of positivism was rejected a priori, the determination of the causes of social phenomena had to be approached from a different standpoint. The answer was found in the method of Verstehen, or sympathetic human understanding. As Raymond Aron explains, German sociologists on the whole "would probably accept Weber's statement that a statistical relationship, however well established, does not satisfy our curiosity and that we desire to understand the link between motives and the act, which will explain human behaviour and the statistical relation itself."[5]

The major thrust of Weber's work was, therefore, an attempt to overcome the clash between positivism and idealism, between the natural and the social sciences, and to synthesize them in his Verstehen approach to sociocultural phenomena. This constitutes his major methodological and theoretical contribution to the social sciences. His ultimate conclusions concurred with those of Windelband, Rickert, and Dilthey; the natural and the social sciences are different in nature. In the natural sciences, man's interest is essentially directed toward prediction and control; he who knows the universe can master and harness its materials and energies for his own ends. In the social sciences, on the other hand, man's interest is essentially directed toward understanding and valuation.

Epistemologically and methodologically, Weber was profoundly influenced by the thought of Kant, Windelband, Dilthey, and Rickert, but, philosophically, Marx and Nietzsche made the deepest impact on his central ideas. Thus he states:

> One can measure the honesty of a contemporary scholar, and above all of a contemporary philosopher, in his posture toward Nietzsche and Marx. Whoever does not admit that he could not perform the most important parts of his own work without the work that these two men have done swindles himself and others.

Our intellectual world has to a great extent been shaped by Marx and Nietzsche.[6]

Weber reacted so sharply to Marx for so long that Albert Salomon contended Weber was "engaged in a life-long dialogue with the ghost of Marx."[7]

Weber's own system was launched by a criticism of two basic and interrelated Marxist theses: the monocausal approach to human history, which interprets the economic relations of production and distribution as the determining factors of the social system; and the notions that ideas are epiphenomena, a superstructure, as it were, of more basic material interests.

To counter these theories, Weber suggested a multicausal approach to human history and to social phenomena and proposed to investigate the manner in which ideas become effective forces in human history and society. Moreover, for Weber, as well as for Robert Michels, Werner Sombart, and Ferdinand Toennies, whom he knew well, the utopian Marxist vision of a full and democratic participation of the proletariat in the social and political process at the culmination of the socialist revolution was doomed to remain a romantic dream of an intellectual professor; continuous growth in population made a bureaucratic structure an indispensable reality. This bureaucratic structure, he claimed, would inexorably subordinate the masses to its apparatus. Thus a true democratic participation in its creation and operation would be an impossibility.

The logic of rationalization, Weber's most fundamental concern and the central theme of his work, links him, dialectically, not only with Marx but also with Nietzsche. For Weber, as for Nietzsche, the universal quest for an answer to the problem of human suffering, for a mythological and then a rational theodicy, is the beginning of philosophical and scientific thought. Both thinkers see the beginning of this process in elaborate theological and mythological cosmogonies and anthropologies and its end in the full emancipation of rational and scientific thought from all religious beliefs and ethics, and in the concomitant loss of the inherent meaning and beauty of life, which gives way to a disenchantment with the world.

Finally, Marx looked at ideas essentially in terms of their function in the class struggle and as originating in the economic substructure, but Nietzsche looked at them in terms of their function for the self-realization of the individual—of the "Great Man"—and as originating from within the depths of the human soul.

Weber looked to epistemology to provide the necessary philosophical foundation for the development of a systematic body of social science to demystify the vague claims of those who control the institutions of society. He also tried to show both the impossibility of making value judgments in the name of science and the impossibility of scientifically establishing a hierarchy of values. He turned to sociology to demonstrate the relativistic nature of all social institutions and organizations as well as the fact that each institution or form of social organization is but *one* among many and, therefore, that none can claim a value superiority on scientific grounds. Finally, he turned to history to furnish the necessary materials to construct a systematic sociology. Honigsheim concludes:

> And thus from epistemological agnosticism and social relativism, Weber built a platform of negativity upon which the human hero ought now to become active—but not just for the sake of empty activism. He ought to be unrestrained by any metaphysic of the state or other untenable ideas, but not, however, by sociology. He ought not to be a utopian but rather a pragmatic politician.
>
> For that purpose sociology ought to be of assistance. Not that sociology should preach about the goals of human evolution or of one's activities, but rather sociology should say: If you want this form of organization, then, under given conditions, you must choose such and such means; further, when you use these means under given economic, foreign policy, or other conditions, then, in addition to the sociological consequences that you want, such and such side-effects of a sociological nature occur. . . .
>
> If one is aware of these two meanings that sociology had for Max Weber, the negative meaning that charges organizations with having a purely relativistic character, as well as the positive meaning which offers the human hero the weapons for battle, then the apparent contradictions that we saw in him are resolved. Moreover, one grasps that this man battled from a position of dualistic metaphysics precisely because he was not a utopian but rather a pragmatic politician and, because of his asceticism, had to embrace a godless science that could give him an answer to none of the ultimate questions. He had to become a sociologist in order to realize his highest goals.[8]

Max Weber can thus be seen as a tragic hero of the intellect who persisted in acting heroically in a nonheroic age. Like one of the knights of Sir Walter Scott or of the *Chanson de Roland*, driven by a great passion for justice as well as for truth, he sought power, essentially through the mind expressing itself by the word, to right wrongs where he saw them, to defend the oppressed, to elevate his nation and his people to a greater role in the modern world, and to present a new ideal of the modern human hero. Thus one of his disciples in Munich aptly compared him to Durer's characterization of the *Medieval Knight*, "sans peur et sans reproche," without fear or favor, taking a straight path between power and the devil.

But Weber was not only a scientist and a politician, a professor and a philosopher, a universal genius and an intellectual of the fin du siècle, he was also, in spite of his denials, a charismatic man, a prophet. Like Comte and Durkheim, but unlike Pareto, he felt he had an important task to accomplish for his nation. H. H. Gerth and C. W. Mills say that Weber really projected "an image of himself" into his characterization of certain Hebrew prophets, particularly that of Jeremiah; and he saw many similarities between the plight of ancient Israel and that of modern Germany. They claim, moreover, that his wife, Marianne, also saw this interesting projection and they concluded that "by interpreting the prophets of disaster and doom, Weber illuminated his own personal and public experiences."[9]

Lewis Coser also came to the same conclusion: that Weber "saw himself in a role similar to that of the Old Testament prophets." Unlike the prophets, however, Weber was unable to "promise his people a better future were they to change their course." Weber, he claims, believed that the future for Western man would be a new ice age where the supreme mastery of a rationalized and bureaucratized way of life would lead to a "parcelling out of the soul." Only occasionally did Weber hope for the emergence of a new charismatic leader who might "arise to lead his people out of the cage of the future."[10]

Although at times, and in his own heart, Weber felt destiny had made him a prophet, and in spite of the fact that many of his students and colleagues felt his charisma and asked for his leadership, Weber always disclaimed publicly that he was a prophet. His task was essentially that of understanding and awareness: to become conscious of his own being and existential situation, of the history and destiny of his own nation, and to lead others to this consciousness. He saw himself as a debunker of myths and ideologies, a Cassandra warning of the impending disaster threatening his nation and Europe as a whole. While Marx sought to convert people to his own views and to prepare the advent of a socialist revolution, Max Weber was more likely to disillusion his listeners and to suggest that reason, honesty, and stoicism were the only noble and truly human attitudes to take toward life and history.

Relatively little is mentioned by Weber's biographers and students about his youth and adolescence. Emilia Souchay, Weber's maternal grandmother, reports that at two and a half, the young Weber was already perfectly self-sufficient and utilized all kinds of objects to build things reflecting the images that had made an impression on him—thus pointing to a very early manifestation of one of his most distinctive features. At the age of four, Weber almost died of meningitis, a disease to which some authors trace the aetiology of his later breakdown. Weber remained a weak and sensitive boy who felt far more at home with books and in the world of the intellect than in the world of daily affairs or that of the rough play of his peers.

A key factor in Weber's life, in the formation of his personality as well as in the formulation of his philosophical and ethical views, was the unhappy relationship between his mother and his father. Helene Fallenstein and Max Weber Sr. had profound personality clashes and deeply opposed value standards. Helene was a religious, saintly, and puritanical woman; Max was a man-of-the-world and a pragmatist who had little use for an ascetic and demanding morality.

The basic incompatibility between the pious and saintly Helene and her pleasure-loving and despotic husband made a deep impression on the young and sensitive Max Weber, and left its lifelong imprint on his personality and values.

Mitzman showed that the fact that Weber had to choose, while he was an adolescent, between the value models of his mother and father had a profound impact on his character and his ethical formulations. This choice, he says, was a major contributing factor to his voluntaristic stand on values, to his insistence on a strictly personal responsibility for one's positions and actions, and to his distinction between an "ethic of responsibility" and an "ethic of success."[11]

A good part of Weber's inner anguish and psychological disturbances came from the fact that, although he knew he should follow his mother's ethic, he followed his father's early in his life and was later never completely able to reject it. Thus he separated *Erfolgsethik* (his father's ethic of success) for his public life and *Gesinnungsethik* (his mother's ethic of conscience) for his private life, with the result that he lived in a state of almost constant tension.

One of the most important lessons Weber learned about life was the necessity for personal experience in order to understand something. This conviction had a double effect on Weber. First, he studied Hebrew to read the Old Testament in its original version, and, second, he lost interest in religion because he could not relate experientially to it—at least as it was expressed in traditional terms and taught in Sunday school. This lesson also, when later fully articulated, laid the foundation for his method of Verstehen.

Having finished his gymnasium program in the spring of 1882,

Weber left home to attend the University of Heidelberg. There he took up law to follow in his father's footsteps, as well as a number of courses in philosophy, history, and economics, which were taught by eminent scholars. At the age of nineteen, after having completed three semesters at the University of Heidelberg, Weber was drafted into the army and moved to Strassburg. Military training proved to be difficult and painful, although sobering and widening, for the young Weber. The year he spent in the Alsatian city, moreover, proved crucial to the formation of his character as well as to the formulation of his axiological foundation and basic philosophical dualism and individualism.

In Strassburg, Weber spent a great deal of time with his uncle Hermann and Aunt Ida Baumgarten. Ida had a deep emotional influence on the development of Weber's personality and on the crystallization of his values; through her he came to understand and to sympathize with his mother and her religious values. Through Ida, Weber also became acquainted with the theologian William Channing, whose moral philosophy and attitude toward religion left a lifelong imprint on him. From Channing, Weber distilled a moral and political philosophy, claiming that true morality and intellectual freedom are products of neither the satisfaction of instinctual urges nor of blind obedience to custom, but, rather, they involve rational self-control and conscious sacrifice of selfish and hedonistic desires for the sake of the higher self and the common good.

The Baumgartens, in short, became a second father and a second mother to the young Weber and, as such, they reinforced, at a deeper and more mature level, his own unfolding value models.

> Throughout his life Weber was to be haunted by another Either/ Or, which was superimposed on the first [his mother's saintliness and piety and his father's worldliness and hedonism]. With ruthless logic he drew as the ultimate radical consequences of Channing's ethic—and his aunt's and his mother's—the Tolstoian refusal, based on the Gospel of Brotherhood, of all cooperation with evil. He never lost respect for this position and accepted it as an ultimate value for personal life; but the man who read as a boy and who never forgot Machiavelli's praise for those Florentines who risked their immortal souls for the salvation of their City also never ceased to maintain against the Tolstoian ethic 'the worldly values ... the active hero-ethic, the service for impersonal cultural possession' which elevate life in this world.[12]

Weber completed his studies at the University of Berlin and, later, at the University of Göttingen. When defending his thesis, after a long and heated debate, Weber received the following eulogy from the great historian Theodor Mommsen: "When I have to go into my grave, I would gladly say to no other than the highly esteemed Max Weber: My son, here is my spear, it is becoming too heavy for my arm."[13]

Already at this point in his life, Weber articulated a multicausal theory of social phenomena and of the unfoldment of the historical process. He saw two main sets of causes for the decline of the older aristocratic-patriarchal system of East Prussia just then being widely debated in Germany: economic causes, resulting from the entry of Germany into the world market, and psychological causes, which he saw as even more important, resulting from the Junkers' need to compete with the life style of urban entrepreneurs and from the farm workers' need for self-liberation from an obsolete patriarchal system. In 1893, Weber married Marianne Schnitger, a distant niece who had come to live in Berlin, and replaced Jakob Goldschmidt in his chair of Commercial Law at the University of Berlin.

In the fall of 1894, Weber was appointed to a full professorship at the University of Freiburg, which he readily accepted. There he became personally acquainted with Hugo Munsterberg, Pastor Naumann, and Wilhelm Rickert, who exerted a profound intellectual and methodological influence on him. In Freiburg as in Berlin, Weber worked compulsively, beyond his natural capacity of endurance, telling Marianne that: "If I do not work until one O'clock I cannot be a professor."[14]

In 1896, Weber accepted the chair of the retiring professor Knies at the University of Heidelberg and moved to that city, the citadel of academic liberalism and democratic philosophy. The inner contradictions of his tormented soul, his family ambivalence, and the inhuman work schedule he had imposed on himself for several years, came to the foreground with the death of his father in 1897 and culminated in his own prolonged nervous breakdown.

Although Weber seemed to have recovered from his initial breakdown, managing to teach a few courses at Karlsruhe and finishing his winter semester at Heidelberg in 1898, he felt completely incapacitated and finally had to resign his teaching position. For the next four years, Weber was to suffer from acute exhaustion, anxiety, tensions, and sleeplessness; he lost his inner balance and his nerves gave way. Gerth and Mills say that Weber suffered intermittently from severe depressions "punctuated by spurts of extraordinarily intense intellectual work and travel," and that he was "held together by a profound sense of humour and an unusually fearless practice of the Socratic maxim."[15]

Around 1901, under the beneficent effects of relaxation and long travels, Weber began to recover gradually, although with intermittent lapses, and he resumed his habit of omnivorous reading. The following year, he felt strong enough to return to Heidelberg to undertake a light work program. In 1904, he accepted the position of associate editor, with Werner Sombart, of the *Archiv für Sozialwissenschaft und Sozialpolitik*, and, through this position, Weber reestablished his social and intellectual contacts with the academic community. Weber also took a trip to America where he was greatly impressed by the New World and its form of capitalism. He was so impressed by what he saw that later, in 1918, he wrote to a colleague that Germany should adopt the American "club pattern" as a means of educating the German masses. He became convinced that putting pressure on the individual to prove himself was a far better way of "educating" than the authoritarian practices of German institutions.

From 1906 to 1910, Weber became deeply involved intellectually with such eminent men as his brother Alfred Weber, Eherhard Gothein, Wilhelm Windelband, Georg Jellinek, Ernst Troeltsch, Karl Naumann, Emil Lask, Friedrich Gundolf, and Arthur Salz. Because of Weber's efforts, the German Sociological Association was founded in 1908; and, in the same year, the University of Heidelberg opened a social science section in the Academy of the Sciences.

When World War I broke out, Max Weber was fifty years of age and declared impulsively that it was a "great and wonderful war" and that he wanted to fight the enemy at the head of his company. Instead, Weber was appointed a captain in charge of nine hospitals in the Heidelberg area. This experience provided, through "Verstehen," the proper existential understanding of a major concept of his sociology—bureaucracy.

In the fall of 1915, Weber retired with an honorable discharge from his army duties. He played the role of an Old Testament prophet of doom to the German authorities, as well as that of an economic expert. At the end of the war, he was appointed as a consultant to the German Armistice Commission in Versailles and contributed to the drafting of the Weimar Constitution.

Turning down a number of positions at the universities of Berlin, Göttingen, and Bonn, Weber went in the summer of 1919 to Munich as the successor of Brentano. In June of 1920 Weber died of an advanced stage of pneumonia, after having published his last lectures under the title of *General Economic History*.

Max Weber the man, the philosopher, and the politician was an incarnation of twentieth-century reason. The power and lucidity of his thought awakened the reasoning faculties of those with whom he came in contact. His ideal as a teacher was not to influence others through the authority of his superior erudition but, rather, to help them unfold their own critical faculties by his example. According to Karl Jaspers, "He can never become the object of a cult, but only the exemplar of a rational man for all who wish to be rational and free, and to understand themselves. In a unique way, he inspired courage, showing the way which, after him, man can and should follow."[16] Jaspers concludes:

> He calls us to seek the truth for ourselves in communication as we advance through time, not to look for ready-made truths to accept and to admire. In failure he hands on the torch, freedom to freedom. The race of men born in the world of Homer and the Jewish Prophets did not die with Nietzsche. Its last great representative so far has been Max Weber. . . . To us who knew him he is a living presence; to others he will always embody the best, the freest type of German, the authentic German.[17]

Weber's Theory of Human Nature, and His Conception of the Ideal Man: Their Interplay With His Life, Thought, and Work

Max Weber was a social philosopher in quest of understanding what it means to be a person in the modern world. Weber spent about three decades studying past and present, religion and law, economics and politics. In seeking to grasp the distinguishing features of western civilization and to understand human behavior from within its own motivational structure, Weber laid down the foundation of a humanistically oriented sociology.

Besides being a social philosopher, however, Max Weber was a jurist and an economist, an historian and a student of comparative religions, a moralist and a prophet of sorts, and a teacher and a politician. But, above all, he was a great humanist, individualist, and rationalist who embodied the best of the German idealistic tradition. He sought to bring to consciousness and to rationally systematize the contradictions of his own thwarted nature, as well as the tensions and antinomies of his young struggling nation, in order to synthesize them into a grand encyclopedic system reminiscent of the great systems of the early and middle nineteenth century. He wanted to know as much of the psycho-social and sociocultural reality as possible, in order to see how much truth he could bear to know. He was an "éveilleur de consciences," who sought to awaken the conscience, both of his nation in a political and historical sense and of his students in a moral and human sense. He was a modern embodiment of the classical Greek philosopher whose highest good lay in rationality and self-mastery.

Weber developed a stern and rigid conscience in his youth. He was disenchanted with the promises of the Enlightenment and horrified by the unleashing of irrational forces both within the souls of men and through the parliaments of nations. He was bound to become a tragic hero, a modern Prometheus seen by some as the "last of the human heroes" and by others as the "oracle of the German soul." To ac-complish his self-appointed mission, to fulfill himself and obtain knowledge about human beings and their conduct, Weber became a social scientist. "Weber's own work is the realization of his self-image as a cultivated man concerned with all things human."[18]

Like Auguste Comte and Emile Durkheim, Weber came to the conclusion that in order to know himself, he must of necessity reconcile and systematize his knowledge of human nature with his knowledge of society. Self-knowledge, a systematic understanding of the nature of man, necessitated the development of the twin perspectives of human biography and of social history. Thus Max Weber, who had to become a social philosopher to satisfy his deepest need and to realize his highest ideal, established the discipline of sociology, in its humanistic and historical interpretation, precisely in order to fuse these two perspec-tives and to thereby gather the information necessary to answer his most fundamental question: What am I? What is man? How can I help man perfect himself? Max Weber had a deep hunger, at the conscious, subconscious, and superconscious levels, to know man in order to improve and perfect him, beginning with himself but then with others as well.

Above all, however, the driving force in Weber's life was the quest for truth, a progressive development of his consciousness enabling him to understand human experience in all its possible configurations. Weber projected this deep need of his and of his epoch into the science of sociology, thus liberating it from the natural sciences. But Weber was not only driven by a theoretical quest for truth, he was also moved by a practical quest for self-realization. Although he sharply distinguished action from knowledge, he did not regard knowledge as an end in itself. Rather, like his predecessors and contemporaries, he held that knowl-edge and understanding were necessary for the perfection of human nature and, through human nature, of the society with which human nature stood in a dialectical relationship.

The theoretical edifice Weber erected on a scientific and historical foundation would serve, he thought, essentially to clarify the issues, to dispel the myths and self-delusions, and to clear the ground for a genuine realization of man. It would show the nature, the scope, and the limits of knowledge in order to enable man's will and values, his god or demon, to break through undistorted to lead him to the unfoldment of his faculties and to the completion of his being. His quest for truth led him in the direction of science and of sociology in particular, and his quest for self-realization led him in the direction of ethics and politics, which, as a good neo-Kantian, he saw as belonging to a qualitatively different dimension.

Although Weber anchored his entire sociological edifice in the individual man as the fundamental unit and ultimate social reality, he, like Comte, Durkheim, and Pareto did not elaborate an explicit and systematic theory of human nature. Implicit in his philosophical, epistemological, methodological, and ethical-political statements, however, looms a theory of human nature which can easily be conceptualized. Weber's varied and comprehensive studies contain intimations of his view of human nature. From these, as well as from his entire intellectual system, I shall attempt to delineate Weber's conception of human nature and, later, his conception of the ideal man.

Weber, as a great humanist and individualist, was unquestionably fascinated by man, whom he considered his greatest and most important object of study. Steeped in the humanistic tradition and deeply committed to its great ideals, Weber could easily have said with Alexander Pope that "the proper study of mankind is man." With St. Augustine, Weber would have agreed that "man wonders about the restless sea, the moving waters, the infinite sky but forgets that, of all wonders, man is the most wonderful, that of all treasures, man is the most precious." And with Goethe, he could well have said that:

> Common folk and world transcender,
> They confess and they agree:
> Highest good life could engender
> Is man's personality.[19]

Like many social scientists and social philosophers of his time and ours, Weber looked at man essentially as a dualistic being who, ultimately, remains an enigma. Weber was influenced in this view by his readings of Goethe and Kant, and from talking with Dilthey and Rickert. Man is both a biopsychic and a psychosocial being, with physical as well as human needs; but behind the animal and the human part of man, stands the great, undefinable and unfathomable mystery of man's spiritual nature and being.

For Max Weber, much like George Mead and unlike Charles Cooley, the self of man exists in a state of tension with the roles he is compelled to play in society. More specifically, the potentially charismatic energies and aspirations of man clash with the external demands of social life; this is reflected in the antinomy between charisma and reason.

Weber's theory of human nature was fashioned in part from an elaboration and refinement of the central postulates and conclusions of Kant, Windelband, Dilthey, and Rickert—by the German idealistic and humanistic tradition—which he sought to fuse with scientific positivism in the hope of establishing a truly scientific and humanistic discipline of sociology. It was also in part derived from his own background, personality structure, and existential experiences.

Weber's theory of human nature, like Comte's and Durkheim's, rests on three basic assumptions. First, a theory of human cognition delineates the nature, scope, and limits of human knowledge. Second, a structural theory outlines man's fundamental dimensions and characteristics, indicating how man became what he is and what he may become in the future. Third, a theory of eudaemonia indicates how man can unfold himself, actualize his human potentialities, and perfect his being.

Thus, a theory of human nature rests on what man is today and on what he hopes and strives to become tomorrow. Human knowledge, human nature, and human destiny, the three fundamental concepts of a theory of human nature, can be seen as resting on the twin foundations of what man is and has achieved today (the static part) and of what man conceives of and labors to realize in himself tomorrow (the dynamic part). It rests, in other words, on present knowledge, experience, and achievements, and on the ideals for the man of tomorrow—on a conception of the ideal man.

Weber's theory of human cognition can be briefly summarized. First, empirical reality, as well as the vaster spiritual reality of man and the world, is infinite, inexhaustible, and unfathomable, both intensively and extensively, that is, man can never become aware of and understand more than a fragment of the reality that makes up both his own being and the world in which he lives. Both man and the world remain, to a large extent, unknown by the limited human consciousness. The sphere of the known may be expanded into the sphere of the unknown, but the unknown, being infinite and inexhaustible, is ever destined to remain larger and wider than the former which can be and must remain but a selective fragment of it.

Second, intellectual systems, based on concepts and theories, do not represent a copy or an image of the empirical reality they purport to portray, but a selective portion of it to which they orient knowledge, understanding, and action. Thought systems, whether scientific, philosophical, or religious, are partial, incomplete, and selective orientations toward reality, which, in its totality, is forever beyond man's grasp. Hence, that empirical reality is the primary source of the "real" and not man's ideas or concepts of it, which are mental constructs designed to orient consciousness and action to certain segments of that reality.

Third, all thought systems can yield only a relative and incomplete knowledge and understanding of the outer and inner reality. All knowledge and understanding are dependent on a priori values or ideals that Weber sees as constituting the core of man's personality and of human societies, which are the guiding and selecting principles through which a fragmentary knowledge of reality is obtained. This is what Weber meant by his key concept of "Wertbeziehung," or value-orientation; that which is considered real and important is loved or desired and constitutes the fundamental categories of the understanding. Man's basic ideals and values constitute a fundamental a priori component of all knowledge and understanding and must, therefore, be accounted for and articulated analytically in order to grasp the orientation, scope, and limits of the knowledge and understanding man is seeking to acquire through his investigations of reality.

Fourth, man must limit himself to empirical knowledge and existential understanding, since his senses, reason, and cognitive processes cannot delve deeper than this form of human consciousness to validly fathom noumenal reality. Hence, scientific knowledge is empirical knowledge and experiential understanding exclusively.

Fifth, knowledge and understanding are separated from ideals and values by an unbridgeable chasm; ideals and values are the result of different faculties and different levels of consciousness than are knowledge and understanding. Knowledge and understanding are the products of observation, cognition, and experience, while ideals and values are the product of the creative will and of the breakthrough of charisma.

Sixth, man's objective knowledge can be essentially of two types: *knowledge ab extra*, or scientific knowledge derived from observation, reasoning, calculation, and experimentation; and *knowledge ab intra*, or Verstehen, understanding derived from a lived human experience or from an empathetic relation to human experience.

Thus, scientific knowledge is the fundamental form of knowledge gathered by the natural sciences, which systematize and organize the characteristics and relationships of objects, and, understanding is the distinctive form of human knowledge gathered by the social sciences, which endeavor to understand the behavior in terms of motivations and conscious orientations, which are, ultimately, based on fundamental values.

This idealistic theory of human cognition, essentially pluralistic and "open," contrasts to the positivistic theory, which is basically monistic and "closed." Hence, the idealistic theory relativizes and demystifies some of the most cherished premises of the positivistic approach, for example, when empirical science will be complete, man will know the world (empirical reality) in its entirety and will be in a position to organize it and to control it rationally; the progress of science is unilinear, ever expanding the domain of the known into that of the unknown; and a scientific ethics and a scientific politics, a scientific solution to the problem of human conduct will eventually be possible and be the greatest achievement of the social sciences.

Weber's structural theory presents man basically as a twofold edifice with, however, a door opened to the unknown and pointing toward a genuine inner spiritual dimension.

First, man is a biopsychic being, who has a biological organism that emerged at the forefront of biological evolution, after millions of years of slow development through the entire animal kingdom. Man's biopsychic organism has become what it is today, for Weber, basically through a superior adaptation to its environment, through a struggle for biological survival.

Weber, however, did not consider man's biopsychic organism to be the essence of his being or the level that harbored his distinctively human characteristics. This was reserved for the next two levels, which, together, represented the seat and structures of consciousness, which Weber saw as embodying man's true essence. Human consciousness constituted the center of Weber's preoccupations and investigations; it was the fundamental object of sociological inquiry and Weber equipped sociology, both methodologically and theoretically, to cope with it. Finally, human consciousness makes possible the dimension of Verstehen, which endows the social sciences both with their unique character and with their superiority vis à vis the natural sciences.

Weber, as a good Kantian, subdivided human consciousness into two basic and heterogeneous dimensions: the cognitive-emotional and the conative-ethical—the sphere of knowledge and sensibility and the sphere of the will and of ideals. These constituted what might be called man's psychosocial being. Weber saw this part as the product of society and history, of sociocultural unfoldment, as he had seen man's biopsychic organism as the result of biological evolution. Thus, man's biopsychic organism can be explained, in its nature, development, and present status, by the natural sciences—biology, zoology, and psychology—while man's psychosocial being can be explained, in its development and fundamental characteristics, by the social sciences—sociology, history, and anthropology.

Above these two levels, but actualized only in a few persons, Weber saw yet a third level, the level of charisma, of creative inspiration, of what I would call the spiritual dimension of man. Charisma constitutes, for Weber, the ultimate mystery and essence of man and the sacredness and ineffability of his personality. Charisma fascinated Weber, and he turned more and more to it at the end of his life, but, in my opinion, he only managed to understand it dimly. For Weber, man's creative will and inspiration, his "gift of grace," or spiritual nature, moreover, was a dimension sui generis that could not be reduced either to biopsychic or to sociocultural factors and, therefore, it could not be explained either by the natural or by the social sciences.

Social science, and sociology in particular, could observe and investigate the historical manifestations and sociocultural implications of charisma, but it could neither grasp its essence nor its source. In spite of the fact that Weber came, at the end of his life, to regard this dimension of man as the taproot of all cultural institutions, the mainspring of sociocultural change, and as the fountainhead of all human thought, he could not fathom its nature or develop a rational system to account for it. This spiritual dimension, for him, was peculiar to *the individual* and was unique in its expressions through the individual. It is as much transcultural as it is transbiological and transpsychological, while, at the same time, having profound physical, psychological, social, and cultural effects. It is the essence and the mystery of the individual; it makes the "individuum" "ineffable."

Charisma manifests itself biopsychically as the vertical breakthrough of a higher dimension in man, of what we would call the "superconscious," and it expresses itself socioculturally as the horizontal breakthrough (the essence of religion) that transforms and propells forward the sociocultural system. Although man's psychosocial being is basically a sociocultural product or "precipitate," man's spiritual nature enables him to become a creator and a maker of society, culture, and history.

Unfortunately, Weber never went further than postulating the existence of the spiritual nature and potentialities of man and studying its historical, social, and cultural manifestations. He never sought to articulate this dimension more fully. I claim that this dimension, and this dimension only, through a qualitative expansion of human consciousness, can explain and bring true understanding of the most vital questions and the ultimate dilemma of man, society, and history.

Weber never truly developed a theory of the spiritual nature of man—as Bergson, Jung, Sorokin, and Eliade attempted. He merely pointed in that direction and stopped at its threshold. His theory of charisma was, perhaps, more an articulation of his strong individualistic, idealistic, and aristocratic positions—with which it "fitted in" nicely and had a profound "Wahlverwandschaft"—than a genuine exploration and development of the spiritual dimension of man and life. Yet, it does provide a good foundation and fertile point of departure for those who are so inclined. Contrary to Bergson's, Jung's, Sorokin's, and Eliade's assumptions, as well as mine, Weber's ingrained pessimism led him to see the charismatic dimension of man as ultimately smothered and extinguished by the world and its everincreasing rationalization rather than overcoming it and transforming it. Also, because of his pessimistic Calvinistic bias, he saw it as becoming rarer in the modern world rather than eventually more prominent.

In his quest for knowledge and for self-realization, Weber also had a deep longing for a spiritual quest, a hunger for truth; his enormous erudition and his lifelong and highly diversified investigations provided a platform to clarify his, and our, basic thinking and premises, to exorcise pseudospirituality and then to proceed toward a genuine spirituality and its systematic study, something he was not able to accomplish in his own life and work.

Weber's theory of eudaemonia is quite simple: each man must become aware of and align his consciousness with his inner daemon and follow its dictates. In other words, man should deliberately cultivate and unfold the powers of his consciousness, his reason and rational capacities, his sensibility, and his willpower. Man should become sensitive to the inner dictates of his being, consciously forge and objectify the ultimate values, ideals, and principles that constitute the core of his character, and which must conform to his own needs, life style, and inner strivings. Finally, he should implement and realize these against all the resistances of his lower nature and of his social milieu, no matter what was the price; only in this way, by making his own soul his truest and greatest "work of art," can man become an authentic human being.

In a sense, Weber's theory of self-realization is akin to the Greek view that the superior man, the philosopher, emerging from the school of "physis" and working his way through the "ethos" of his society, should unfold his human potentialities to the point where he can become aware of the indwelling "logos" and become capable of following its dictates through thick and thin.

Weber's fundamentally aristocratic position led him to see the masses of men as "children" or half-developed humans whose lives, thoughts, feelings, ideals, and actions remained structured by the external forces of society or by the subliminal drives of their own being. The great man, the fully developed human being, on the other hand, is no longer the tool and product of society and history, but is their master and creator. Rather than remaining a "parceled out soul" in a bureaucratic organization or a "little cog" in the big machine of modern industrial society, the fully actualized man can comprehend and control these forces for his own ends by understanding and mastering, first of all, himself. Weber claimed man could, at his best, become aware of these thousand and one strings that pull his soul and, especially, that he could become aware of the supreme ideal that would free him from being the instrument of his instruments. Having become aware of his supreme ideal, man should then patiently, heroically, and, perhaps, tragically, try to fashion his human consciousness, his character and life, around this ideal, from within the sphere of his conscious ego.

Underlying Weber's theory of human nature and, indeed, underlying his entire intellectual system as well as his major methodological and theoretical developments, stood his conception of the ideal man—of what the good, the authentic, and fully actualized human being should be, which, on account of his far-reaching dualism, was a double one. In spite of its intrinsic complexities and antinomies, Weber's twin conception of the ideal man, and how this conception permeated and subtly influenced his entire thought, his life, and actions, is fairly clear. The ideal is that of the puritan ascetic and rationalist scientist on the one hand, and of the charismatic prophet on the other.

Weber never quite resolved and integrated this dual and contradictory ideal in his life and work, but, ultimately, he reconciled it in his conception of the cultured and well-rounded man, the "Kulturmensch," who is the specialist in one field and well-versed in many fields, who is capable of understanding and responding to the entire spectrum of human experience, and who sees and feels himself to be what Weber himself had termed in his youth the "Ich Weltmensch."

Weber was quite aware of his double conception of the ideal man and of the influence of this conception on his methodological and theoretical developments as well as on the course of his life. A cardinal assumption of his intellectual system is precisely that all knowledge is oriented toward certain facets of reality by values and that unless a person were conscious of these value-orientations, he could never become truly aware of the nature, scope, and limits of his research and of the data and conclusions it presented.

Of all the fundamental ideas and conceptions devised by the human mind, the most general and important are those of God, man, society, and the world, on which one's entire *Weltanschauung* depends, and which are peculiarly related to each other by an inner logic. Weber spent many years of research to show how ideas and ideals affect human behavior and, in particular, how religious ideas affect economic behavior, that is, how the idea of God and man affects action in society and in the world.

Weber's personal temperament and general disposition influenced his twin conception of the ideal man. Weber was hypersensitive and had been grievously ill with meningitis, which, according to some medical opinions, further intensified his sensitivity and intelligence. Weber had a powerful nature—volcanic passions on the one hand and a keen intellect on the other; he had a deep need to know and understand objectively and an equally deep hunger for action, for self-assertion and self-expression. Finally, his health also played a major role throughout his life, with recurrent periods of enforced inactivity followed by periods of extraordinary stimulation and productivity, thus preventing him from realizing some of his most cherished ambitions and ideals and generating a frustrating helplessness as well as a gap between the visions of his mind and his capacity to realize them.

Next, Weber's family background—the sharply opposed ethics and example of his mother and father—embodied two contradictory ideals and life models. The fact that his mother and father had incompatible characters, that they were both highly articulate and deeply committed to their own ways and ideals, and that they repeatedly clashed with each other had, as Mitzman and others have pointed out, a deep and lasting effect on the formation of Weber's personality, Weltanschauung, and major ideals. Here, perhaps, as psychoanalytically oriented thinkers would claim, are the roots to many tensions in Weber's psyche and intellectual system. Central among these is, perhaps, Weber's fundamental and ubiquitous view of life as a struggle, as an inevitable and ongoing battle, his radical individualism, his equally radical and omnipresent dualism, his pluralism and polytheism, and his total cognitive rejection of "Werturteile" or value judgments, from science and from sociology in particular.

Together with his family background, and further intensifying and bringing into the foreground of his consciousness the clash between his mother's and his father's values and ideals, were the adolescent experiences he had with his Aunt Ida and his Uncle Hermann Baumgarten in Strassburg at a crucial point of his life. Some students of Weber's life and work have gone as far as claiming that it was through the influence of Ida and Hermann that Weber finally got to appreciate his mother's value model in its true light; this led him to veer away from his father's without, however, ever being able to fully reject it or to cut himself off from the latter, either emotionally or intellectually.

Finally, the sociocultural system in which Weber lived influenced the formation of his character, the crystallization of his Weltanschauung, and the definition of his major assumptions and ideals. Having been born into a highly cultured upper-middle class family with an active and cosmopolitan social life, having traveled extensively and studied, as well as taught, at some of the leading German institutions of higher learning, Weber, who was endowed with an insatiable curiosity and with keen powers of perception, was profoundly and painfully aware of the traditions, problems, and issues with which Germany struggled. He internalized these tensions to an unusual extent, seeking to reconcile them and to give the best of himself to his nation—to enhance its power as well as its moral, intellectual, and scientific stature.

At the sociocultural level, therefore, Weber encountered in his young and struggling nation the confrontation of old traditions with new ways, the clash of idealism with positivism, of science with religion; he saw the agony of the old aristocratic tradition and the abrupt and bewildering rise of the bourgeois capitalist class; he experienced the opposition between the nationalists and conservatives on the one hand, and that of the internationalists and socialists on the other; he contemplated the highly efficient bureaucracy of the state with an incompetent leader; finally, he saw the coming of World War I with its emotionally exhilarating stimulus and its intellectual forebodings of disaster and "Götterdämmerung." All of these sociocultural strands were fully and consciously absorbed by Weber who, as an ancient Titan and Demiurge, wrestled with them within his own breast. A student who had keenly observed this rightly compared him to "a giant resurrected warrior from the forests of Germany, in whose hands an unwarlike age had pressed a pen instead of a sword . . . a Duke who moved into battle at the head of his vassals."[20] All these dimensions, sets of forces, and influences entered into the formation of his psyche and into the articulation of his intellectual system.

Weber's first conception of the ideal man left a deep imprint on him for the rest of his life. Weber saw the puritan, or Calvinist, as the emerging model of the man who had fashioned the modern industrial cosmos in which he lived. It was the "inner-worldly ascetic," who, for Weber, from a given conception of God, of man, and of nature, had fashioned the world of science, technology, capitalism, and had made the bureaucracy in which he had to live.

In observing and meditating on the world, that is, the sociocultural system in which he lived, and in seeking to understand it, Weber went back to understand the kind of man who had created it and identified with it, consciously or unconsciously seeking, in his own life and person, to bring this man to his fullest possible level of development and realization. The "Kulturtraeger," the carriers and examples of this type of man, Weber found in his mother and in her sister Ida, and in her spiritual mentor William Channing. In these people, Weber found distilled the quintessence and the concrete embodiment of the Puritan variety of Calvinistic asceticism, which he sought to make his own and to articulate. This ethos, carried to its logical extreme, led him to his mental *surménage* and to his eventual breakdown, from which he was never able to completely recover. It is from these people, too, that he began to appreciate the ethical position he would later call "Gesinnungsethik," the ethic of ultimate ends. In his grandfather, Karl A. Weber, Max Weber also found a living, concrete personification of the early type of capitalist he had found in his readings and which he considered to be at the root of the modern industrial society.

In his father, on the other hand, Weber found a countermodel, intellectually as well as existentially, an opposition both to ascetic rationalism and to the ethic of ultimate ends of his mother. In his father, Weber found the easygoing sensualist, the representative of the ethic of success, of opportunism, and of the search for power; he found the bureaucratic submission to the authority of superiors and the tyrannizing of inferiors—of his mother in particular, against which he was to rebel so violently and tragically later in his life.

In his uncle Hermann, Weber found what was to become for him the model of the honest and conscientious professor who had not sold out to the establishment and who was keenly aware of his own value orientations as well as of those of others; he found the countermodel to Treitschke, who personified for him all the traits he most despised in academicians, strong support of the establishment and the use of the academic chair as a platform to expose the personal political views he hoped to inculcate in others.

The first and deepest crystallization of the ideal man Weber sought to become and to express in his life is undoubtedly that of the Calvinist Puritan, that of the inner-wordly ascetic, which he saw as having emerged both within his family, and, historically, within his society, as the current form of the good and fully actualized man standing at the forefront of the sociocultural evolutionary forces. This person, by his own strivings and efforts, by his own existential experiences and sufferings, forges his character as a work of art, as a refined instrument with which to work on and to transform the outer world according to his own will and ideas. This person sees the phenomenal world, especially in its sociocultural aspects, as the product of human wills and ideas; the ideal man, having known and mastered himself, now proceeds to know and to master the physical world to serve his own needs.

But man, the rationalistic scientist, bureaucrat, and entrepreneur, in his great concentration on obtaining mastery and power over his biopsychic and instinctual self and in his Promethean efforts to harness the natural resources and energies of the world, has forgotten and betrayed the receptive and feminine part of his nature; he has renounced or repressed his emotional life and his ability to love. It is love, intuition, and faith, which alone can, ultimately, provide true meaning, a sense of purpose, and happiness in life; the Calvinist Puritan now lives in a meaningless, purposeless, and loveless world, in a world that has emasculated and unbalanced human consciousness, stripped it of its capacity for feeling, for being receptive to higher spiritual energies; he now sees the world as disenchanted. This man, from this level of human consciousness and from this existential position, sees the future of humanity in the following terms: "Not summer's bloom lies ahead of us, but rather a polar night of icy darkness and hardness, no matter which group may triumph externally now."[21]

The Calvinist Puritan, the man of will and reason and of the Prussian "verdamnte Plicht," whom Weber internalized through the teachings and example of his mother and her sister, can direct man's concentrated energies on two great tasks at two different levels. He can seek to master himself, to offer a trained and responsive instrument to the divine will, or he can seek to master the natural resources and energies of the world to transform it into the Kingdom of God, that is, into the likeness of his own ideals and conceptions of what it should be. Moreover, he can direct his concentrated efforts on the goal of seeking to gather knowledge of the world and understanding of man (the theoretical part accomplished through the natural and the social sciences), or, on the goal of transforming the real into the ideal, that is, of perfecting man's being and man's environment (the practical part accomplished through technology, industry, and bureaucracy directed by politics).

The end result of this conception of the ideal man, embodied and enacted by a particular type of human personality, is a thoroughgoing rationalization of man's consciousness, of his conception of, and relationship to, the world. As Weber himself vividly puts it:

It means . . . the knowledge or belief that, if one but wished one could learn it at any time. Hence, it means that principally there are no mysterious incalculable forces that come into play, but rather that one can, in principle, master all things by calculation. This means that the world is disenchanted. One need no longer have recourse to magical means or implore the spirits, as did the savage, for whom such mysterious powers existed. Technical means and calculation perform the service. This above all is what intellectualization means.[22]

This first conception of the ideal man, which Weber later transformed by reintroducing and emphasizing the emotional and spiritual side of human nature, but which he was never able to fully reject, had a profound and lifelong influence on the formation of his personality, on the course of his life, and on the articulation of his intellectual system.

To begin with, it imbued Weber with one of his deepest passions and endowed him with the distinctive feature of his character, his deep-seated hunger for truth, his unquenchable need to know and to understand, his encyclopedic and titanic strivings to explain man's actions, the nature of man, and the world in which man acts. This passion for truth led Weber to his first career or vocation, that of science; science, in turn, led him to his "verstehende Soziologie."

Weber's ideal led him to deny his powerful emotions and instincts for a long time. Eventually the denial exacted a costly price and a painful revenge on his psyche. He worked compulsively and above his power of endurance, which resulted in a series of nervous breakdowns and in prolonged periods of inactivity as well as in his vast erudition and detailed studies covering half a dozen professional fields, and in his systematic but unfinished "understanding sociology." He studied society and history to understand himself and to project his self-knowledge and self-understanding into a generalized and universalized knowledge of man, of human society, and of social action. He studied the Protestant ethic and, later, other religious ethics in order to grasp within a large cultural perspective the nature and origins as well as the material and social consequences of this ideal he had made his, and which he saw as having emerged as the ideal of the modern world. Finally, he articulated, in part, the individualism, dualism, nominalism, and pluralism that were the foundation of his intellectual system.

This axiological foundation led Weber to formulate his basic criteria for what constituted a good scientist and an authentic man; both form an elite, the first an intellectual elite, the second an ethical aristocracy. Concerning science and the good scientist, who is an offshoot of his first conception of the ideal man as the "inner-worldly ascetic," Weber wrote: "Science today is a 'vocation' organized in special disciplines in the service of self-clarification and knowledge of interrelated facts. It is not the gift of grace of seers and prophets dispensing sacred values and revelations, nor does it partake of the contemplation of sages and philosophers about the meaning of the universe."[23]

Science, in other words, is solidly anchored in the phenomenal and experiential world, and it must, therefore, thoroughly purge itself of all metaphysical concepts; it must renounce all investigations and explanations of the ultimate reality it is powerless to grasp. Moreover, as it can grasp only a finite number of general and individual features of the empirical world, it is an endless quest ever to be superseded by future generations. Finally, it must differentiate sharply between value judgments and ideals, which come from another sphere beyond its reach and, therefore, are not its legitimate domain, on the one hand, and facts and value orientations, on the other. As Weber himself concluded: "The intellectual constructions of science constitute an unreal realm of artificial abstractions, with which their bony hands seek to grasp the blood-and-the-sap of true life, without ever catching it."[24]

What then can science contribute to modern man according to Max Weber? "First, of course, science contributes to the technology of controlling life by calculating external objects as well as man's activities. . . . Second, science can contribute . . . methods of thinking, the tools, and the training for thought. . . . [Third, and most important, science helps us] to gain clarity."[25]

Science can thus offer man intellectual clarity about himself, his goals, and his activities, as well as the most rational and efficient means whereby to reach his stated goals and to calculate their costs and consequences.

The authentic man, following the Weberian conception, is, therefore, the man who understands himself, the nature and limits of human knowledge, the nature and dynamics of the world, both physical and sociocultural, and who is the master of himself and of his environment. He must forge and fashion, from the depths of his own inner being, the ultimate values and ethical principles to guide his life and determine his earthly destiny. In a sense, he is not a flesh and blood reality, he is not a biopsychic, psychosocial, and spiritual being, but an intellectual abstraction, a Promethean figure who, though socialized into a given sociocultural milieu and aware of the values and norms of his society, has risen above them and has transfigured them in the depths of his being.

Weber's second vocation, that of politician, aimed at transforming the world. The politician needs not only knowledge and understanding of human nature, of the dynamics of society, and of the art of politics, but also he needs passion and power. For Weber, the true politician or statesman stands at the polar opposite to the scientist or the civil servant. Thus, generating a central antinomy within his first conception of the ideal man and a dialectical relationship between its two formulations, Weber writes:

> [The Civil servant shall execute his duties] *sine ira et studio,* without scorn or bias, he shall administer his office. Hence, he shall not do precisely what the politician, the leader as well as his following, must always necessarily do, namely fight.
>
> To take a stand, to be passionate—*ira et studium*—is the politician's element and above all the element of the political leader. His conduct is subject to a different, indeed, exactly the opposite principle of responsibility from that of the civil servant.[26]

The preeminent qualities of the ideal man of action, of the true statesman, are, for Weber, passion, a keen sense of reality and of proportion, and, especially, a sense of responsibility for his own actions.

Weber also linked the image of the good politician, the man of action who enters the world of charisma, with Old Testament Prophets. And he found "elective affinities" between himself and these Prophets, whom he described so vividly. In them and in their distinguishing emotional and intellectual features, he sees himself, as his wife recognized in reading his notes.[27] Weber identified with Isaiah and with Jeremiah in particular, but he might have unconsciously projected some of his own distinguishing traits onto their personalities.

Weber's strivings for completion, for synthesis and reconciliation of the existential paradoxes and antinomies of human life and of his own being, however, made themselves felt even in his double articulation of the inner-worldly ascetic as a man of reason and reflection and as a man of action and passion. Toward the end of his address, "Politics as a Vocation," he sought to find a meaningful bridge between a commitment to an ethic of ultimate ends and a commitment to an ethic of responsibility.

However, it is immensely moving when a mature man—no matter whether old or young in years—is aware of a responsibility for the consequences of his conduct and really feels such a responsibility with heart and soul. He then acts by following an ethic of responsibility and somewhere he reaches the point where he says: "Here I stand; I can do no other." That is something genuinely human and moving. And everyone of us who is not spiritually dead must realize the possibility of finding himself at some time in that position. In so far as this is true, an ethic of ultimate ends and an ethic of responsibility are not absolute contrasts but rather supplements, which only in unison constitute a genuine man—a man who can have the "calling for politics."[28]

Despite the fact that Weber deeply believed that the modern industrial world, produced by the Protestant ethic and the rationalizing effects of science, had created an intellectual climate which made it impossible for prophets and seers to appear, he still longed for a genuinely charismatic man to appear and to lead modern man out of his present existential impasse. Moreover, he conceptualized this spiritual man as his second and supreme ideal for man which, in a sense, he strove to become almost in spite of his rational, Calvinistic self. Hence he writes, showing that, in spite of the emphasis on reason and modern science, genuine spirituality still exists:

The fact of our times is characterized by rationalization and intellectualization and, above all, by the 'disenchantment of the world.' Precisely the ultimate and most sublime values have retreated from public life either into the transcendental realm of mystic life or into the brotherliness of direct and personal relations. It is not accidental that our greatest art is intimate and not monumental, nor is it accidental that today only within the smallest and most intimate circles, in personal human situations, in *pianissimo*, that something is pulsating that corresponds to the prophetic *pneuma*, which in former times swept through the great communities like a fire-brand, welding them together.[29]

After his nervous breakdown of 1899-1903, after he had experienced the ultimate consequences of driving himself beyond his capacities, Weber stated that he then felt as though "an icy hand had let him loose" and that the emotional and feminine part of his being had been reawakened in him. Later, through his long and diversified investigations of religion, he became aware of another homo religiosus, the exemplary prophet which now becomes, in his eyes, the purest form of the charismatic, or spiritual, man who provided the nucleus of his second conception of the ideal man.

Max Weber came to the conclusion that man can reach God, the source and essence of all being, life, and goodness by two basic paths: that of the ascetic and that of the mystic. The first path, in its theoretical aspect, leads inevitably toward science and, in its practical aspect, toward politics—toward the modern world of rationalization and bureaucratization, of technology and industry with its systematic and precise knowledge of the empirical world and the harnessing of its energies and raw materials for physical comfort. But it also leads, equally inevitably, toward a loss of meaning and purpose in the world, toward a loss of *joie de vivre* and a *raison d'être*. It leads toward an atrophy of the female and receptive faculties of man, of emotion and intuition, of love and faith.

The second path, however, leads toward spiritual knowledge and understanding of reality, of man's true being, purpose, and destiny in the world, in its theoretical aspect, as well as toward the actualization of his spiritual nature, faculties, and consciousness in its practical aspect. It leads toward a living communion with the essence of being, life, and love, toward joy and ecstasy. It leads toward a detachment from the things of this world and toward an attachment to the things of the spirit. It leads to what the mystics call "passing from the unreal to the real, from death to life, and from man to God." Mysticism, moreover, was also seen by Weber as being closely related to aristocratic views he held throughout his life.

Weber, according to Mitzman, sees mystical illumination as a distinctive religious quality of the upper classes. This is because "being," rather than "doing," is a central feature of both the mystical experience and of the aristocratic ethos. He claims, moreover, that for Weber there is a "psychological correlation of both mystic and aristocratic ethics with exemplary prophecy and of the ascetic and plebian with ethical prophecy." "The ethical prophet," he writes, "rooted in the ascetic plebian code of transcending a reality filled with pain, preaches a rational morality of subservience to the will of an all-powerful, transcendental deity, in whose service men are mere 'instruments' for the realization of his commands. The exemplary prophet, like the mystic and the aristocrat, does not preach, but simply offers his own standards of 'Being' which is this kind of prophet's condition of contemplative possession of the Divine, as a model for those who would follow him."[30]

Science can provide a systematic and precise but relative knowledge of the material and empirical side of life, social science can provide an understanding of man and of his human experience, but neither can provide absolute knowledge and understanding of the noumenal, or spiritual, reality that constitutes the essence of both material and human reality. Technology and industry can harness the energies and resources of nature to put them to the service of man and to render his life more comfortable. Politics can lead toward national power and expansion. But none of these can provide any true meaning and purpose for man's being and life; none can lead man toward either the solution of the riddle of the sphinx, the mystery of life, and the enigma of the universe, or toward the unfoldment and realization of his consciousness and being.

For Weber this meant that, ultimately, the human will and reason were not ends in themselves but merely instruments toward faith, love, and an intuition which are a genuine charisma, a breakthrough of something higher into human consciousness. And, therefore, ultimately, the mystic is superior to the ascetic just as the will and reason ultimately depend upon faith, love, and inspiration for their fulfillment. The source of all being and reality, the roots of human freedom and creativity, can only be disclosed by a charismatic breakthrough.

Weber well recognized this even at an early stage in his career, namely that science and reason cannot create and dictate true ideals and ends for man; they merely show him the best and most efficient means by which he can realize the ends obtained by use of different faculties. Ends are obtained subconsciously from the social system by the immature and unrealized man-child and obtained superconsciously from an inner logos by a charismatic breakthrough by the realized and mature man. Weber also recognized that charisma is not the product of either the human will or reason, or human efforts or genius, but, rather, the breakthrough into human consciousness of higher spiritual energies and states of consciousness, the revelation of the sacred, the theophany of man's true Self which is received by the feminine faculties of love, faith, and inspiration.

The ascetic, therefore, whether of an inner-worldly or other-worldly type, is not the truly charismatic man, he is not the fully developed and realized man; rather, he merely represents a step toward that end, a means to prepare the way for a genuine breakthrough of divine grace. The ascetic may have received a genuine inflow of charisma at one time but then rationalized this breakthrough and continued to pursue its existential implementation by a systematic application of his will. While his will and reason are prevalent over his faith and love, he remains closed and unreceptive to a continuous and progressive breakthrough of divine grace.

Thus, the second and supreme Weberian conception of the ideal man is the true charismatic man, the exemplary prophet; this person, through love and faith, has established a continuous inflow of spiritual inspiration in his own psyche and acts as a channel through which spiritual light and energies are released into his community and into the world. In conscious contact with the source of his own being and life, as well as with the source and essence of reality, this person is able to bring a sense of meaning, of purpose, and of ultimate ends into this world for himself and for those who are willing to follow him. It is the man who preaches by his own living example, by the drawing power of his own light, truth, and wisdom, and by what he *is* rather than by what he *does.* He imposes no categorical imperatives on others, but leaves them free to follow his example through love and faith rather than through coercion or intimidation. By his own being and example, the charismatic person leads others to actualize the best that is in them, to find the supreme law of their being, to discover their own higher selves. It is the man who shows others by what he is now, by the light and power of his gift of grace, what they, too, may become in the future and whose greatest incarnation was Jesus of Nazareth.

Weber himself, however, was not a mystic, or the exemplary prophet he saw as his last great ideal for man and as indispensable for the salvation of the modern world. Weber remained essentially a man of will and reason, an inner-worldly ascetic, the Calvinist rationalistic puritan of his youth. He sought, however, more and more to free himself from the burden of his youth and destiny; he could mentally conceive of the freeing grace of faith and love, emotion and intuition, of the surrender of the self to a higher self, but he could not achieve this ideal existentially. He remained, therefore, a great, suffering, and universal genius, an anguished and passionate man who could not integrate the fundamental dichotomies of his conceptions and ideals—the male and female aspects of his being, his ascetic and mystical tendencies, reason and passion, theory and practice, an ethic of responsibility and an ethic of ultimate ends, and his public and private life.

Weber remained torn within himself, in constant tension and conflict, and could only prefigure cognitively the higher spiritual integration of his self that would have brought peace, joy, and fullness of being to his soul. To a great extent Weber projected his own self-image onto the Old Testament Prophet when he wrote of him: "The prophet of doom emerged from his solitude after having experienced his vision and born out his inner conflicts. He returned to the solitude of his home, viewed with horror and fear, always unloved, often ridiculed, threatened, spit upon, slapped in the face."[31] Weber thus remained "menschlich-allzu-menschlich," a living portrait and example of what man is, in the deeper reality of his human nature, torn between his physical and his spiritual nature. An embodiment of the soul of Germany and of the consciousness of Europe, he stood astride two centuries and two worlds, and represented, better than most, the fin du siècle.

Rather than a capitalistic entrepreneur or a great statesman, rather than an ascetic moralist or an exemplary prophet—some of the traits he felt deeply alive and throbbing within his being—Weber remained basically a great individualist and rationalist, a first-class intellectual and a great social scientist, who laid the foundations for a humanistic sociology. Rather than awakening the spiritual nature and faculties of his disciples and intensifying their faith in God, Weber awakened the intellectual powers of his students and friends, stimulated their reason and critical faculties, and inspired a deep reverence for intellectual honesty and objectivity and for social justice and fairness, by the drawing and infectious power of his own brilliant mind and scientific analyses. Thus Max Weber appealed to and brought out the distinguishing traits of man's human nature, rather than those of his animal nature, or those of his spiritual nature; and, as such, he may rightly be viewed as a modern Prometheus, or as an éveilleur de consciences.

Even though Weber did not arrive at a full articulation of his twin conception of the ideal man as an inner-wordly ascetic and as an exemplary prophet in his own life, even though he did not succeed in fully reconciling and integrating the two facets of his ideal of the inner-worldly ascetic, he did succeed in formulating a concept that could embody the various antagonistic features of his ideal of man, and he did succeed in incarnating and living this self-image to some degree. This concept of the cultured, civilized, and well-rounded man became his self-image and practical ideal toward the latter part of his life.

This conception of the "Kulturmensch," or well-rounded humanist, stood in direct opposition to that of the "Fachmensch," the specialist and narrow expert whom Weber saw as inexorably rising in the modern world as the type of personality corresponding to the way of life it imposed. This conception, moreover, brought Weber to somehow attempt a synthesis—even if an unstable and precarious one— between his twin and opposed concepts of rationalization and charisma, and to stand ultimately, particularly in his private life and in the innermost recesses of his being, on the side of charisma, in spite of the fact that, objectively, he saw charisma as vanishing from the world in which he lived.

Behind his concept of rationalization stands his ideal of the Calvinist Puritan, the man with a sober intellect and an iron will, just as behind his concept of charisma stands his ideal of the exemplary prophet, the man of faith and love who, through his gift of grace, can penetrate into and comprehend the essence of reality, of humanity, and of human destiny. Behind his concept of Wertbeziehung, behind his insistence on keeping value judgments separate from facts, behind his demand for restricting scientific knowledge to empirical and experiential data, and for intellectual honesty and objectivity stood his twin conception of the ideal man as a man of will and reason and as a man of faith and love with a gift of grace.

Behind his insistence on the strict separation of theory from practice, of reason from passion, and of an ethic of responsibility from an ethic of ultimate ends, stood the essential Kantian dualism, which he incorporated into his conception of what man is and of what man ought to be. Finally, behind his famous three-fold typology of legitimate authority and his conception of charisma as the central motor of sociocultural change and the ultimate source of the great human values that crystallized into social institutions, stood his vision of a genuinely charismatic man as the true leader of men and as the model of the full and authentic man of the future.

Max Weber, and his life and work, furthermore, are a living witness to his ideal of, and strivings to become and remain, a cultivated and well-rounded man in the modern world. Everything that has ever been thought, felt, or experienced by any human being, was interesting to him. Thus, at the root of Weber's psyche and human consciousness, at the heart of what he was and of what he strove to become, as well as at the axiological foundation of his thought and intellectual system, lie his great values and ideals, his conception of what man was, of how he became what he is, and of what man should ideally become. He would have said that the essence of the human personality is what man knows, what he loves, and what he strives to become, just as the core of the sociocultural system is composed of the great values and ideals around which it crystallizes. To understand man, as well as human societies, we must know what they conceive to be real, to be true, and to be important and desirable.

Max Weber, the founder of "understanding sociology," the great and tormented professor of Imperial Germany, the last of the encyclopedic minds of the modern social sciences, and the last of the human heroes, did not complete his Promethean search nor did he achieve his last great ideal of man as a genuinely charismatic or spiritual man, but he did light a flame in the social sciences and he passed on to us the torch of the quest for truth and of the quest for self-realization; it is now up to us to keep that flame alive and to bear this torch nobly and to carry on where he left off.

6

CONCLUSION

My investigation of the lives, sociocultural milieus, and intellectual systems of four selected social theorists has revealed that the quest for self-knowledge and the quest for self-realization were central motivational drives behind their academic endeavors, as well as major structural elements of their personal lives and thought. My study showed these men to be genuine humanists of the Western intellectual tradition and, at the same time, it vindicated the classical assertion that "know thyself" provides the conscious or unconscious core of such tradition. I found, moreover, that this injunction became articulated and systematized, in their works, through a theory of human nature which was undoubtedly the structural and axiological kingpin of each intellectual system. In each case I found that it was the key assumptions and central insights of the theory of human nature with its conception of the ideal man that undergirds the theory of the nature of society, the theory of the nature of history, and the conception of their own major discipline—sociology. I found, furthermore, that the former stands in a dialectical relationship to the latter such that they mutually influence each other. I also found that there is a profound dialectical relationship not only between each theory of human nature and its conception of the ideal man and each intellectual system, but also between each theory of human nature and each personal life.

At the analytical level, their theories of human nature prove to be composed, structurally, of three major sets of assumptions or conceptions: a conception of man, of what man is today in terms of what he was yesterday, and of man's distinctive characteristics; a conception of human knowledge, of what man can know and how he knows, and of the genesis, dynamics, and distinctive features of human knowledge; and a conception of how man could actualize his human faculties and potentialities, and become a fuller being, that is, a theory of eudæmonia underpinned by a conception of the ideal man.

This theory of human nature with its implicit conception of an ideal man, moreover, was studied and interpreted within the context of the authors' intellectual systems as wholes, seen within the perspective of their personal lives and within the framework of the sociocultural system in which each lived and of its Zeitgeist. My investigations clearly show how these central dimensions—the writer's personal life, the sociocultural milieu in which he lived, his intellectual system, and his theory of human nature with its conception of an ideal man, emerging within it both infrastructurally and axiologically, formed an indivisible, dynamic whole, the structural parts of which are interconnected. Thus my study corroborates, at a specific and concrete level, the central teaching of the sociology of knowledge, that is, that social existence and human thought are deeply intertwined and mutually affect each other in such a way that neither could be properly understood without the framework provided by the other.

The central hypothesis of this book—that the key concepts and basic orientation of social theories and of their methodologies are subconsciously, preconsciously, and consciously influenced by an implicit or explicit, by an embryonic or articulated, conception of an ideal man—was demonstrated concretely in each particular instance. In short, I show how Auguste Comte, Emile Durkheim, Vilfredo Pareto, and Max Weber have sought to know and to understand themselves by investigating the nature and dynamics of society. Each projected and reified his own reactions to the crucial issues and problems of his society, thus unconsciously seeking to universalize his own personal experiences. Finally, my study shows how each developed a conception of an ideal man and was then influenced by this conception both for the direction of his personal life and for the development of his social theories and their methodologies.

Social theorists do have certain key "postulations," or "background assumptions," as Gouldner points out, and these are highly important for a proper understanding of the man and his creative thinking. They must be made explicit and accounted for analytically by any serious explanatory model purporting to investigate what social theory is, how it is formulated, what its key structural components are, how it operates, and what its theoretical and methodological strengths and weaknesses are.

The sociology of knowledge can be further advanced by the central insights and conclusions of this book. In differentiating between ideologically tinged thinking and its roots, and socially determined thought and its basic processes and manifestations, the concept of the ideal man, operating behind its author's theory of human nature, is illuminating. The sociology of knowledge shows, on the one hand, the relativity and selectivity of sociological theories, their scientific claims notwithstanding, and, on the other, their deep infrastructural and axiological connection with their author's personal values and biography, located within a given sociocultural matrix. It shows, in other words, that what a theorist observes, studies, and experiences, what he offers by way of understanding and interpretation, is inextricably bound to and refracted by his vision and ideals—by what he loves, by what he considers to be real, important, and desirable, and by what he strives to become. It shows that, at the human and social levels at least, the past and the present, the present and the future, what has been called causality and teleology, form an indivisible and interacting whole, the structural parts of which can only be separated analytically but not existentially, and which must, for valid explanatory purposes, be interpreted in interaction with each other.

My conclusions are the following:

1. The prime motive of the life and work of the four social theorists I studied was their deep desire to know and to understand man in order to improve and perfect him, and this in order to know and understand themselves and to fully actualize their human faculties and potentialities. Thus, these authors became sociologists and investigated the nature, origin, unfoldment, and dynamics of human societies, thereby laying down the foundations of modern sociology. Their agreement was unanimous, with the exception of Pareto in his later works, on the view that man's human nature is a social product, that is, that human consciousness is born, nourished, and expanded through social interaction.

2. The lives and work of all four theorists were characterized by a twin motif: a theoretical quest for truth, and a practical quest for self-realization—with the exception of Pareto, who, later in his life, asserted that all he was interested in was knowing the truth and not in changing anyone or anything. (In any case, according to his system, nothing could be changed.) The quests for truth and for self-realization are expressed, respectively, in intellectual systems, or theoretical scientific endeavors, and in social, political, religious, educational, and moral, or practical endeavors.

3. The quests for truth and for self-realization became conceptualized and systematized, as well as defined, in theories of human nature that rest on conceptions of what man is, conceptions of human knowledge, and conceptions of an ideal man. The theories of eudaemonia suggest ways to realize and to embody these conceptions. The theories of

human nature and the conceptions of the ideal man provide the infrastructural assumptions and the axiological frameworks on which the theories of the nature of society, history, and their conceptions of their disciplines rested, all of which together form the structural skeleton of their intellectual system.

4. A complex set of dialectical relationships exists between the theories of human nature and their conceptions of the ideal man, and their intellectual system, on the one hand, and, on the other, between these two noological dimensions and their personal experiences in a given sociocultural milieu. During their youths and formative years and through crucial human encounters or readings, a certain conception of what man is and of what man should be—of the good and fully humanized and actualized man—emerged. These conceptions and their related assumptions and implications were then woven into their intellectual systems providing their central structural and axiological foundations. Then, in their mature years, these conceptions, with their assumptions and implications, began to "feed back" into and to profoundly affect their personal lives and their unfolding social theories and methodologies, thus completing the dialectical cycle.

5. In each individual case, therefore, including that of Pareto in a negative way, I observed a profound interrelation between the lives of the authors and their thought, both of which were deeply anchored in a given sociocultural system; I observed a profound connection between their theories of human nature with their conceptions of the ideal man and the formulation of social theories and methodologies— the asking and answering of certain questions, the raising and solving of certain problems.

Auguste Comte's theory of human nature was seen to be essentially the following: man is endowed with a biopsychic and a psychosocial nature. He is, therefore, the product of a two-fold evolution: a biological evolution through the animal and the human species, and a social evolution through the unfoldment of history in human societies. The heart of man, for Comte, is not his biopsychic nature but rather his psychosocial nature, which must, therefore, be investigated not by biology but by sociology. Man's psychosocial nature, which is brought out through his human relations, constitutes his genuinely human self, his human consciousness, the distinctive features of which are thought (knowledge), feeling (love), and behavior (action).

The fundamental problem of human nature, which, for him, can only be solved in a social way, is the expansion of human consciousness. Comte wants to increase man's capacity to know and to understand, to feel and to love, and to act and to create in a harmonious fashion and in such a way that knowledge be motivated and oriented by love and that activity be directed by knowledge. The "intelligence" and the "character" should be subordinated to the "heart"; altruism rather than egoism should be the motive power of the heart. The fundamental problem of social life is, therefore, for him, the transformation and purification of the human heart so that egoism be subordinated to altruism or, as he puts it, how to make sociability prevail over individuality. To accomplish this, man needs a very rigorous and thoroughgoing social discipline affecting all of his thoughts, feelings, and activities—which is what Comte's positivism and the religion of humanity will provide.

Comte's theory of human cognition anchors positive, or scientific, knowledge in direct observation and in human experience, both of which are conceptualized and organized by reason. His theory of eudaemonia consists essentially in unfolding and fully realizing man's distinctively human nature, that is, his human consciousness with its three functions. And this is to be accomplished through making man give the best and highest of himself to others in a rich, varied, and regulated network of human interactions.

Undergirding Comte's theory of human nature, at the infrastructural and axiological level, stands his implicit, and later more explicit, conception of the ideal man, the guiding ideal of his entire intellectual system. The ideal man for Comte is the positive man, the sociocentric man who is the knower, lover, and servant of humanity. This "man for others" subordinates his thoughts, sentiments, and actions to humanity. He is the universal man, the Weltmensch, who has actualized his higher social instincts and has mastered his lower personal instincts and inclinations. He is at one with the great being, which is Comte's intellectual reification and projection of the concept of God, who represents the highest and best in actualized human nature.

From his early youth onward, and particularly during his mature years, Comte was in search of ideals to which he could dedicate his life, intelligence, and energies. The greatest of these was the ideal of what he should become, the conception of an ideal man, which he could embody and preach to others. His encounters with Encontre, St. Simon, and Clothilde constituted the crucial human relations enabling him to formulate and to crystallize his emerging ideal of the positive sociocentric man. His philosophical, political, and religious endeavors, his very life and work, since his recovery from his cerebral episode, were an attempt to further articulate, concretize, and actualize this ideal.

Finally, Comte's intellectual system and his various social theories were clearly a grand projection of his theory of human nature onto the canvas of human societies and history, behind which stood, as its integrating and unifying principle, and as its end, his conception of the ideal man living the good life in the good society.

Emile Durkheim saw man, just as Comte did, essentially as a homo duplex, a biopsychic and psychosocial being. Again, as Comte before him, Durkheim saw man's true self as residing in his human nature, his human consciousness, or, in what he knows, what he loves, and what he can do. Human consciousness, for Durkheim, is purely a social creation, an offspring of the conscience collective that gives birth to it, nourishes it, and expands it. Thus, if one wishes to know the heart of man, the structure and expressions of human consciousness, it is necessary to know and understand the society that forged it. Where Durkheim's theory of human nature departs from Comte's, to which it is similar in most respects, is at its roots. For Comte, society and human relations merely elicit or bring out the faculties and potentialities inherent in human nature. Society, in other words, translates preexisting potentialities into manifest realities; it guides man from a being *in posse* to a being *in esse*. For Durkheim, on the other hand, society and human relations actually create and graft onto man's biopsychic nature his human consciousness and its key faculties: rationality, self-mastery, and moral autonomy—the characteristics sui generis of the "creative social synthesis."

The fundamental problem of human nature for Durkheim is also how to fully humanize man. And this can only be accomplished by integrating man within a variety of social groups in order to unfold his distinctively human traits. The fundamental problem of social life, on the other hand, is the insertion of the individual in structured and vital human groups so that he may become more himself as he becomes more "at one with society": it is to make man more social so that he may become more individualized.

Durkheim's theory of human cognition is, essentially, the same as that of Comte but with more emphasis on observation and reflection and less emphasis on love and feeling as noetic faculties. It is a more naturalistic and positivistic theory which asserts that valid scientific knowledge can only come from empirical observation and human experience, which is then conceptualized, organized, and interpreted by reason.

His theory of eudaemonia consists, therefore, in forging, nourishing, and expanding man's human nature, or human consciousness, to the greatest possible extent by "living with and for others," that is, by giving the best and highest of one's self to one's society through varied and regulated social relations.

Durkheim did not have, as Comte did, one universally valid conception of the ideal man, but several. Each society, he claims, will create its own supreme ideal of what man should aspire to and become. For his own society and for himself, however, Durkheim did have a specific conception of what the good, humanized, and socialized man should be. He is the sociocentric man, the man-for-others; he is content with what he is and has; he is fully adapted and adjusted to his sociocultural milieu and in full harmony with the best of his Zeitgeist, being particularly receptive to its noblest and highest aspirations. And the sociocentric man is best represented by the sociologist, who will inaugurate the sociological era.

Since Durkheim views society as the underlying reality behind the concept of God and since he sees society as the father of man's human consciousness—of his rationality, self-control, moral autonomy and dignity—it is logical that, for him, the good man is the sociocentric man, the man that has united and identified his life and being with the creative source of his highest distinctive traits—society.

As one of the most important tasks of modern man is to specialize himself and to work with others, Durkheim saw the sociologist, as the modern and enlightened humanist, moralist, and sociocentric man, as his own personal and supreme conception of the ideal man—to which he dedicated the best of himself, his efforts, and his life. And it is in sociology that his twin quests for truth and for self-realization merged and found their fulfillment.

Durkheim, too, as Comte before him, was in search of ideals to which he could dedicate his life and the best of his efforts and intelligence. And of these, the ideal of what he should become, the conception of an ideal man, was unquestionably the most fundamental. Whether his relationship with Boutroux, Renouvier, and Hamelin or his readings of Kant and Montesquieu provided the crucial experiences enabling him to formulate and crystalize his emerging conception of the sociologist is hard to say. What I can state, however, is that this ideal answered a profound need of the society in which Durkheim lived. Durkheim's mature life and endeavors—his philosophical, scientific, social, political, educational, and religious investigations—clearly constituted an attempt to further articulate, expand, and embody this ideal.

Finally, Durkheim's system as a whole and his various social theories and methodologies also constituted, as in the case of Comte, an articulation and logical development of his dualistic theory of human nature behind which stood his conception of the ideal man as a guiding light and as the supreme end toward which all of his efforts ans aspirations were directed.

For Vilfredo Pareto man is essentially an animal who is fully encompassed by nature and its laws, which he can never transcend. Man is an animal, however, who is endowed with a fringe of rationality and with the desire and the illusion of becoming something higher and nobler than he is and is destined to remain. Man here is not conceived as a homo duplex but, rather, as a unidimensional being, as a biopsychic, nonlogical, and egoistical animal, who, driven by his own internal residues, does not change and cannot change as the centuries roll by. Man, for Pareto, is, therefore, essentially a presocial or, rather, a nonsocial being into whom society can hardly penetrate and much less transform. Human consciousness, which, for the other authors, constitutes the truly human essence of man, is but an efflorescence, an epiphenomenon, of his biopsychic, nonlogical, and egoistical nature. It is, therefore, like the foam at the crest of ocean waves: without causal and creative power; it can know, it can perhaps understand, but it cannot change or improve what man is. Man and human societies, therefore, remain essentially the same, in a state of shifting equilibrium that brings to the foreground different elements, or residues, of human nature.

Pareto's theory of human cognition rests on two basic assumptions: first, scientifically valid knowledge can only be gathered from observational data that are conceptualized, organized, and interpreted by reason. Love, feeling, intuition, and human experience are left out and considered nonscientific, with the result that scientific knowledge is what he termed logico-experimental knowledge. Second, all reality is one, homogeneous, and continuous, without qualitative jumps between the animate and human realms.

These two assumptions, which he borrowed uncritically from his sociocultural milieu, led him to the conclusion that the model by which to represent and analyze all reality is that of rational mechanics. This approach, therefore, became the paradigmatic model that he projected into all of his economical, political, and social studies.

Pareto's theory of eudaemonia aborted, together with his conception of an ideal man, in the midst of its emergence and articulation. In his youth and formative years, Pareto had hoped to understand himself and the society in which he lived by developing a mechanistic, or logico-experimental sociology—by transposing the model of rational mechanics he had learned as an engineer into the study of human nature and human society; he had hoped, in other words, to become a man of science, a man who would seek truth—knowledge of himself and of his society—so as to improve himself and to contribute to the growth of his nation on all levels. He had hoped, moreover, to achieve scientific and political recognition for his efforts; but when his practical efforts failed, his ideals failed with them and so did his theory of eudaemonia. As a result, Pareto did not have a genuine conception of an ideal man but only the vision of a superior man, which he sought to become and did become to a large extent.

Pareto's superior man, the mechanistic sociologist, is a grand inquisitor who dares to look human and social reality in the face. He is completely frank and honest with himself; he will apply the logico-experimental method so as to penetrate to the bedrock of human and social reality and debunk all derivations, ideologies, religions, and ideals. He will dare to see man in all his inhumanity; he is willing to shed all his childish dreams of the goodness and purpose of life, and, for the sake of truth, he will uncover the naked face of human bestiality, of social exploitation, and of the misery that underlies all social existence. In other words, he is thoroughly realistic and disenchanted, seeing man, and himself, at his lowest common denominator—his selfish animal nature.

In his youth and in the formative years of his life, Pareto, too, had been in search of worthy ideals to which he could dedicate his life and the best of himself. Into this search, he poured all the passion of his Latin nature and all his idealism. From his studies, Pareto gathered his rationalistic and mechanistic model for all valid human thinking and from his father, he gathered his early liberal, democratic, Mazzinist ideals—against which he turned so bitterly at the end of his life. But then, when all his practical endeavors failed, Pareto turned against all of his former ideals; he developed and sought to personify his conception of the superior man, of the mechanistic sociologist.

Finally, there is a close fit between Pareto's theory of human nature, with its aborted conception of the ideal man, and his intellectual system. Pareto's social theories are clearly an externalization and an articulation of his theory that human nature is essentially animalistic, irrational, egoistical, unchangeable, without higher faculties, and without a true purpose and destiny. What Pareto did, perhaps without realizing it, was to project onto the world at large his own personal experiences and to universalize them into a treatise of systematic sociology.

Max Weber's theory of human nature, like those of Comte and Durkheim, presents man as essentially a homo duplex, who, however, remains ultimately an unfathomable enigma. Man is both a biopsychic and a psychosocial being; but, behind these two empirical dimensions, lies an undefinable and ineffable mystery of man's spiritual nature, expressing itself through charismatic breakthroughs, which, in the final analysis, define and rule the human world. Man is thus an incomplete being endowed with two natures and undergoing an evolution that might lead to and culminate in a third nature, the spiritual nature. For Weber, as for Comte and Durkheim, man's psychosocial being, his human consciousness, constitute his distinctively human features, and are made the center of his preoccupations and investigations. Human consciousness is subdivided into two basic dimensions: first, the cognitive-emotional, and, second, the conative-ethical, the sphere of knowledge and sensibility and the sphere of the will and of ideals. The first he ascribed mainly to man's social life, to his interactions with his fellowmen; the second he ascribed mainly to the charismatic breakthrough or creative expression of man's inner being. Although man's psychosocial nature constituted the practical focus of sociological research, Weber acknowledged that, in the final analysis, man's spiritual nature constitutes his true essence and endows his personality with sacredness and ineffability.

Weber's theory of cognition was based on three fundamental assumptions. First, reality is infinite and unfathomable, both intensively and extensively. Hence all knowledge must, necessarily, reflect a selective fragment of reality. Second, all knowledge is dependent on the a priori values and ideals that constitute the selecting principles through which such knowledge is obtained. Third, valid scientific knowledge includes only empirical knowledge and existential understanding, because man's senses and reason are inadequate to probe the noumenal dimensions of reality.

The two major conclusions of this theory are: first, knowledge and understanding are separated by an unbridgeable chasm from values and ideals that issue from different faculties; second, valid scientific knowledge is either scientific knowledge derived from observation and reasoning or understanding derived from a lived human experience or from an empathic relation to a lived human experience.

Weber's theory of eudaemonia declares essentially that each human being must become aware of, and align his consciousness with, his inner daemon and follow its dictates; man should wrest from the innermost depths of his being his supreme ideal and the principles whereby it may be achieved; and then man should follow the ideal in spite of all external obstacles.

Underlying Weber's theory of human nature, and, in fact, his entire intellectual system, standing at the infrastructural and axiological level, is his dualistic conception of the ideal man which was the guiding light and the unifying and integrating principle of his life as well as his thought. This conception is briefly that of the puritan ascetic on the one hand, and that of the charismatic prophet on the other. Although Weber never quite succeeded in reconciling these two ideals, toward the end of his life, he did integrate them to some extent in the conception of the cultured and well-rounded man, the Kulturmensch.

The puritan ascetic is the inner-worldly ascetic, the man of will and reason who, by his own existential experiences and sufferings, forges his character into a work of art. Having understood and mastered himself, this person now proceeds to know and to master the physical world. The "lone great man," in short, is the captain of his ship and must forge and fashion, from the depths of his inner being, the ultimate values and ethical principles that will guide his life and determine his earthly destiny.

The charismatic prophet, on the other hand, is the genuinely spiritual man, the exemplary prophet; he is the man of love and faith who has established a continuous inflow of spiritual intuition, and he acts as a channel through which grace is released into the world. In conscious contact with the source of his being and of all life, he can, therefore, bring a sense of meaning and purpose, of ultimate ends, into the world for himself and for those who will follow him. By his own being and example, and the awakening power of his own charisma, he leads others to actualize the best that is in them, to find the supreme law of their being, and to discover their own higher selves.

The cultured and well-rounded man, which Weber succeeded in becoming, to a certain extent, during his mature years, is the true humanist, who has lived through a broad range of human experiences, who has loved passionately and suffered acutely, and who can, therefore, empathize with and understand what it means to be a man in the modern world.

Max Weber, like his fellow sociologists Auguste Comte, Emile Durkheim, and Vilfredo Pareto, had searched deeply and persistently for ideals to embrace and particularly for an ideal to incarnate—for a conception of an ideal man. Through his parents and his relatives, Ida and Hermann Baumgarten, through his personal experiences and his readings, Weber forged for himself the ideal of the Calvinist Puritan, which he sought to embody during the first part of his life. There were far-reaching consequences for his health and his thinking, which he was never able to discard and to fully exorcise. As a reaction to his first conception of the ideal man, as a result of his protracted breakdown and vast readings in the field of religion, and, perhaps, as a result of his meeting some genuinely charismatic human beings, Weber fashioned his second conception of the ideal man—the charismatic prophet, which, however, he was never able to personify. Perhaps as a result of his two contending conceptions of the ideal man, or perhaps because of what he had already lived and become, and of what he felt most in resonance with, Weber formulated his third and last conception of the ideal man as the Kulturmensch.

The impact of Weber's conceptions of the ideal man on his life were considerable. It is largely due to his ideal of the Calvinist ascetic that Weber overstrained himself in his work, unbalanced his psyche, and made his two main vocations science and politics. It is also largely due to his ideal of the charismatic prophet that he studied religion in such depth and breadth; and, lastly, it is largely due to his conception of the Kulturmensch that he developed and understanding sociology and that he articulated his method of Verstehen.

Finally, Weber's intellectual system was deeply affected, both in form and content, by his theory of human nature and his dualistic conception of the ideal man. The major questions he raised and the way in which he went about providing answers to them all reflect his central conception of the ideal man.

In conclusion, the theoretical and methodological foundations of modern sociology were established by men who sought to reconcile and to integrate, in a consistent synthesis, positivism and romanticism, liberalism and conservatism, the faith in reason and in man's perfectibility and its ensuing disenchantment and refocusing on the unconscious and the irrational. These men were scientists, philosophers, reformers, and prophets of a new discipline, a new form of knowledge, and a new world with a new man. They were unmistakably grandchildren of the Enlightenment, offspring of the nineteenth century, and men of the fin du siècle. All wrestled at length with the problem of religion and its place in modern society, and they attempted to formulate a scientific explanation of it. Their erudition embraced many fields and a variety of vocations. Their greatest concern was, ultimately, to explain the nature of man, and his behavior and social experiences in their totality through a synthesis that would integrate science, philosophy, and religion.

For Comte, society is the great being, the true reality behind the religious concept of God, and the source and essence of man's human nature. For Durkheim, society is the central explanatory concept of his system, the source of all man's higher ideas and ideals, and the ultimate source of the sacred. For Pareto, the Italian patrician without illusions, society is the eternal arena of political conflict where a small and organized elite ever rules the large disorganized masses. For Weber, society is the collection of acting individuals with certain goal orientations.

The need for further research, along the lines indicated by this inquiry, appears compelling and tantalizing. Further research could be undertaken along many avenues, but two seem to contain more promise. First, there is a need to study the relationship between the conception of the ideal man and the theory of human nature, and the intellectual system of contemporary sociologists such as Talcott Parsons, Pitrim Sorokin, and Robert Merton, within the perspective of their biographies and sociocultural milieus. Second, there is a need to investigate the psychological, social, cultural, philosophical, moral, and religious implications and consequences of unfolding the conception of an ideal man as a spiritual being—as a genuinely inspired, awakened, and actualized human being, the promise and the ideal held by all great world religions and which yet remains to be concretely and existentially achieved.

These two lines of research should then make substantial contributions not only to a further and deeper understanding of the structure and function of social theories and of the sociology of knowledge, but, more importantly, to modern men currently undergoing deep transformations, acute suffering, and profound soul-searching.

Notes

Chapter 1

1. Alvin Gouldner, *Enter Plato* (New York: Basic Books, 1965), p. 171. Emphasis mine.
2. Ibid., p. 197.
3. Ibid., p. 243.
4. *The Coming Crisis in Western Sociology* (New York: Avon, 1970), pp. 28-29.
5. Ibid., p. 32.
6. *The Sociology of Knowledge* (London: Routledge and Kegan Paul, 1958), p. ix.
7. Ibid., p. 12.
8. *Ideology and Utopia* (New York: Harvest Books, 1936), pp. 39-40.
9. *The Sociology of Knowledge*, pp. 49-51.
10. Ibid., pp. 71-72.
11. *Ideology and Utopia*, p. xx.
12. Ibid., p. 20.
13. *The Sociology of Knowledge*, p. 127.

Chapter 2

1. Lucien Levy-Bruhl, *La Philosophie d'Auguste Comte* (Paris: Félix Alcan, 1921), p. 1.
2. Ibid., p. 2.
3. *Cours de Philosophie Positive*, 6 vols. (Paris: Bachelier, 1842) 4:396-97.
4. Levy-Bruhl, *La Philosophie d'Auguste Comte*, p. 3.

5. Manuel, Frank, *The Prophets of Paris* (New York: Harper & Row, Harper Torchbook, 1965), p. 1.

6. *Psychologie de deux Messies Positivistes: St. Simon et Auguste Comte* (Paris: Félix Alcan, 1905), p. 3.

7. Ibid., p. 5.

8. *The Sociology of Religion*, 5 vols. (New York: Fordham University Press, 1966-72) 1:154.

9. Ibid., p. 140.

10. Manuel, *The Prophets of Paris*, p. 5.

11. Henri Gouhier, *La Vie d'Auguste Comte* (Paris: J. Vrin, 1965), p. 32.

12. Comte, *Cours de Philosophie Positive* 6:ix.

13. Gouhier, *La Vie d'Auguste Comte*, p. 38.

14. *Psychologie de deux Messies Positivistes*, p. 284.

15. Ibid., p. 297.

16. Auguste Comte, *Système de Politique Positive*, 4 vols. (Paris: Mathias, 1851-54) 4:iii-iv.

17. Dumas, *Psychologie de deux Messies Positivistes*, p. viii.

18. *Auguste Comte, The Mad Philosopher* (New York: Random House, 1954), p. iii.

19. *La Vie d'Auguste Comte*, p. 210.

20. *Cours de Philosophie Positive* 3:209-10.

21. *Système de Politique Positive* 3:14.

22. Auguste Comte, *Discourt sur l'Esprit Positif* (Paris: Carilian Coeury, 1843), p. 60.

23. Ibid., p. 86.

24. Ibid., p. 425.

25. Auguste Comte, *Catéchisme Positiviste* (Paris: Félix Alcan, 1852), p. 169.

26. Ibid.

27. *Cours de Philosophie Positive* 1:621-22. *Système de Politique Positive*, 1:716.

28. *Système de Politique Positive* 1:711.

29. *Catéchisme Positiviste*, p. 157.

30. *Système de Politique Positive* 1:716.

31. *Catéchisme Positiviste*, p. 170.

32. *Système de Politique Positive* 1:733.

33. *Catéchisme Positiviste*, p. 172.

34. *Système de Politique Positive* 3:7.

35. Ibid. 1:732.

36. Ibid. 1:626.

37. *Cours de Philosophie Positive* 3:637.

38. Blaise Pascal, *Pensées* (New York: Pantheon Books, 1965), pp. 485-89.

39. *Synthèse Subjective* (Paris: V. Dalmant, 1856), p. 59.

40. *Système de Politique Positive* 1:91.

41. *Système de Politique Positive* 1:8.

42. Ibid., 3:73.

43. *Catéchisme Positiviste*, p. 9.

44. Ibid., p. 266.

45. *Système de Politique Positive* 1:700.

46. Ibid. 4:175.

47. *Catéchisme Positiviste*, p. 21.

48. Ibid., p. 67.

49. Ibid., p. 58.

50. Ibid., p. 177.

51. Ibid., p. 139.

52. *Testament d'Auguste Comte* (Paris: Société Positiviste, 1896), p. 79.

53. *The Prophets of Paris*, p. 293.

54. *La Vie d'Auguste Comte*, p. 162.

Chapter 3

1. *Emile Durkheim* (Englewood Cliffs, N.J.: Prentice Hall, 1965), p. vi.

2. *Durkheim: sa Vie, son Oeuvre* (Paris: Presses Universitaires, 1965), pp. 54-55.

3. *Emile Durkheim*, p. 28.

4. "Auguste Comte et Durkheim," *Revue de Métaphysique et de Morale* (1921) 28:642.

5. Emile Durkheim, *Sociology and Philosophy*, trans. D.F. Pocock (Glencoe, Ill.: Free Press, 1953), p. 34.

6. Emile Durkheim, *De la Division du Travail* (Paris: Félix Alcan, 1926), pp. 459-60.

7. "Emile Durkheim," *Revue de Métaphysique et de Morale* 85 (1919):183-94.

8. *The Fundamental Forms of Social Thought* (New York: Fordham University Press, 1963), p. 243.

9. Kurt Wolff, ed., *Essays on Sociology and Philosophy* (New York: Harper & Row, Harper Torchbook, 1960), p. 4.

10. *Emile Durkheim*, p. 10.

11. Wolff, *Essays on Sociology and Philosophy*, p. 146.

12. Nisbet, *Emile Durkheim*, p. 172.

13. "L'Oeuvre Sociologique d'Emile Durkheim," *Europe*, 15 February 1930.

14. Ibid., p. 297.

15. "Emile Durkheim," pp. 183-94.

16. Harry Alpert, *Emile Durkheim and His Sociology* (New York: Russell & Russell, 1962), p. 17.

17. "Emile Durkheim," p. 28.

18. Bouglé, "L'Oeuvre Sociologique d'Emile Durkheim," p. 298.

19. "Emile Durkheim," p. 194.

20. "L'Individualisme et les Intellectuels," *Revue Bleue* 10 (1898):7-8.

21. Ibid., pp. 9-11.

22. *Emile Durkheim and His Sociology*, p. 69.

23. Bouglé, "L'Oeuvre Sociologique d'Emile Durkheim," p. 299.

24. Ibid., p. 301.

25. Ibid., p. 302.

26. Wolff, *Essays on Sociology and Philosophy*, p. 326.

27. Ibid., p. 327.

28. Joseph Vialatoux, *De Durkheim à Bergson* (Paris: Bloud & Gay, 1939), p. 62.

29. Wolff, *Essays on Sociology and Philosophy*, pp. 327-28.

30. *L'Education Morale* (Paris: Félix Alcan, 1926), pp. 21-23.

31. *De la Division du Travail*, pp. 4-6.

32. *Education et Sociologie* (Paris: Presses Universitaires, 1966), p. 116.

33. Ibid., p. 90.

34. Ibid., p. 91.

35. Emile Durkheim, *Suicide*, trans. John A. Spaulding and George Simpson (New York: Free Press, 1951), p. 213.

36. Durkheim, *L'Education Morale*, p. 119.

37. Ibid., pp. 120-21.

38. Ibid., p. 115.

39. "Sociologie Religieuse et Théorie de la Connaissance," *Revue de Métaphysique et de Morale* 17 (1909):756.

40. *De Durkheim à Bergson*, p. 49.

41. *The Elementary Forms of Religious Life*, trans. Joseph Ward Swain (New York: Free Press, 1965), p. 470.

Chapter 4

1. Stuart Hughes, *Consciousness and Society* (New York: Vintage, 1961), pp. 34-36.

2. *Vilfredo Pareto: sa Vie et son Oeuvre* (Paris: Payot, 1928), p. 16.

3. Giovanni Busino, *Introduction à une Histoire de la Sociologie de Pareto* (Genève: Droz, 1968), p. 11.

4. Ibid., p. 19.

5. Ibid., p. 20.

6. George Bousquet, *Pareto, le Savant et l'Homme* (Lausanne: Payot, 1960).

7. *See* Stark, quoted by James Meisel in *Pareto and Mosca* (Englewood Cliffs, N.J.: Prentice-Hall, 1965), p. 49.

8. Busino, *Introduction à une Histoire de la Sociologie de Pareto* (Genève: Droz, 1968), p. 42.

9. Ibid., p. 12.

10. George Bousquet, *Pareto, le Savant et l'Homme* (Lausanne: Payot, 1960), p. 181.

11. Meisel, *Pareto and Mosca*, p. 54.

12. *Lettere a Maffeo Pantaleoni*, 3 vols. (Rome: Gabriele de Rosa, Edizioni de Storia e di Letteratura, 1962) 1:141.

13. *The Mind and Society*, 4 vols. trans. Andrew Buongiorno and Arthur Livingston (New York: Dover, 1963) 2: S850-51.

14. Ibid., S875.

15. Ibid., S888.

16. Franz Borkenau, *Pareto* (New York: Wiley), p. 33.

17. *The Mind and Society*, S1249.

18. Ibid., S1301.

19. Ibid., S1419.

20. Ibid., S1687.

21. *See* S.E. Finer in Vilfredo Pareto, *Sociological Writings* (New York: Praeger, 1966), p. 82.

22. *The Structure of Social Action* (Glencoe, Ill.: Free Press, 1961) 2:283.

23. Pareto, *The Mind and Society*, p. S2080.

24. *Lettere a Maffeo Pantaleoni* 3:252.

25. Ibid. 1:xvii.

26. Ibid. 3:19.

27. Pareto, *The Mind and Society*, S2191.

28. Pareto, *Lettere a Maffeo Pantaleoni* 1:54.

29. Ibid. 3:436.

Chapter 5

1. *The Iron Cage* (New York: Knopf, 1970), pp. 3-4.

2. Karl Jaspers, *Three Essays* (New York: Harcourt Brace & World, 1968), pp. 256-57.

3. Blaise Pascal, *Pensées* [my translation] (New York: Pantheon Books, 1965), p. 412.

4. S.M. Miller, *Max Weber* (New York: Thomas Crowell, 1964), p. 4.

5. *German Sociology* (Glencoe, Ill.: The Free Press of Glencoe, 1967), p. 109.

6. Quoted by Mitzman, in *The Iron Cage*, p. 182.

7. Miller, *Max Weber*, p. 7.

8. Paul Honigsheim, *On Max Weber* (New York: Free Press, 1968), p. 133.

9. H.H. Gerth and C.W. Mills, eds., *From Max Weber: Essays in Sociology* (New York: Oxford University Press, 1967), p. 27.

10. Ibid., p. 78.

11. Mitzman, *The Iron Cage*, p. 35.

12. Mitzman, *The Iron Cage*, pp. 11-13.

13. Quoted in ibid., p. 13.

14. Quoted in ibid., p. 17.

15. Gerth and Mills, *From Max Weber: Essays in Sociology*, p. 33.

16. *Three Essays*, p. 261.

17. Ibid., p. 273.

18. Gerth and Mills, *From Max Weber: Essays in Sociology*, p. 73.

19. Quoted by Werner Stark, *The Fundamental Forms of Social Thought* (New York: Fordham University Press, 1963), p. 247.

20. Mitzman, *The Iron Cage*, pp. 174-75.

21. Gerth and Mills, *From Max Weber: Essays in Sociology*, p. 128.

22. Ibid., p. 139.

23. Ibid., p. 152.

24. Ibid., pp. 140-41.

25. Ibid., p. 142.

26. Ibid., p. 95.

27. Ibid., p. 27.

28. Ibid., p. 127.

29. Ibid., pp. 154-55.

30. Ibid., p. 243.

31. Max Weber, *Ancient Judaism,* trans. H. H. Gerth and D. Martindale (New York: Bedminster, 1967), p. 293.

SELECTED BIBLIOGRAPHY

Primary Sources

Comte, Auguste. *Appel aux Conservateurs.* Paris: Auguste Comte, 1855.

————. *Catéchisme Positiviste.* Paris: Félix Alcan, 1862.

————. *Correspondances Inédites d'Auguste Comte.* Paris: Société Positiviste, 1904.

————. *Cours de Philosophie Positive.* 6 volumes. Paris: Bachelier, 1830-42.

————. *Discourt sur l'Esprit Positif.* Paris: Carilian Coeury, 1843.

————. *Lettres d'Auguste Comte à Divers.* Paris: Société Positiviste, 1896.

————. *Synthèse Subjective.* Paris: V. Dalmant, 1856.

————. *Système de Politique Positive.* 4 volumes. Paris: Mathias, 1851-54.

————. *Testament d'Auguste Comte.* Paris: Société Positiviste, 1896.

Durkheim, Emile. *De la Division du Travail.* Paris: Félix Alcan, 1926.

————. *Education et Sociologie.* Paris: Presses Universitaires, 1966.

————. "Introduction à la Morale." *Revue Philosophique* 45 (1920).

————. *L'Education Morale.* Paris: Félix Alcan, 1926.

————. "L'Individualisme et les Intellectuels," *Revue Bleue.* 31 December 1898.

————. *L'Evolution Pédagogique en France.* Paris: Félix Alcan, 1938.

————. *Montesquieu and Rousseau.* Ann Arbor: University of Michigan Press, 1966.

————. *Pragmatisme et Sociologie.* Paris: Librairie Philosophique, 1955.

————. *Socialism and St. Simon.* Translated by Charlotte Sattler. Yellow Springs, Ohio: Antioch, 1958.

————. *Sociology and Philosophy.* Translated by D.F. Pocock. Glencoe, Ill.: Free Press, 1953.

————. "Sociologie Religieuse et Théorie de la Connaissance," *Revue de Métaphysique et de Morale* 17 (1909).

————. *Suicide.* Translated by John A. Spaulding and George Simpson. New York: Free Press, 1951.

————. *The Elementary Forms of Religious Life.* Translated by Joseph Ward Swain. New York: Free Press, 1965.

————. *The Rules of the Sociological Method.* Translated by Sarah A. Solonay and

John H. Mueller. Chicago: University of Chicago Press, 1938.

Pareto, Vilfredo. *Les Systèmes Socialistes.* 2 volumes. Genève: Droz, 1966.

———. *Lettere a Maffeo Pantaleoni.* 3 volumes. Roma: Gabriele de Rosa, Edizioni di Storia e di Letteratura, 1962.

———. *The Mind and Society.* Translated by Andrew Buongiorno and Arthur Livingston. 4 volumes. New York: Dover, 1963.

———. *Mythes et Idéologies.* Genève: Droz, 1966.

———. *Oeuvres Complètes.* 8 volumes. Genève: Droz, 1966.

———. *Sociological Writings.* Translated by Derick Mirfin. New York: Praeger, 1966.

Weber, Max. *Ancient Judaism.* Translated by H.H. Girth and D. Martindale. New York: Bedminster, 1967.

———. *Basic Concepts in Sociology.* Translated by H.P. Secher. New York: Citadel, 1969.

———. *Economy and Society.* Translated by Ephraim Fishoff et al. 3 volumes. New York: Bedminster, 1968.

———. *From Max Weber: Essays in Sociology.* Edited by H.H. Gerth and C.W. Mills. New York: Oxford University Press, 1967.

———. *On Charisma and Institution Building.* Edited by S.N. Eisenstadt. Chicago, Univesity of Chicago Press, 1968.

———. *The Sociology of Religion.* Translated by Ephraim Fishoff. Boston: Beacon, 1968.

———. *The Protestant Ethic and the Spirit of Capitalism.* Translated by Talcott Parsons. New York: Scribner, 1958.

Secondary Sources

Albert, Harry. *Emile Durkheim and His Sociology.* New York: Russell & Russell, 1961.

Aron, Raymond. *Les Etapes de la Pensée Sociologique.* Paris: Gallimard, 1967.

———. *German Sociology.* Glencoe, Ill.: Free Press, 1967.

Bendix, Reinhart. *Max Weber: an Intellectual Portrait.* New York: Doubleday, Anchor Books, 1962.

Borkenau, Franz. *Pareto.* New York: Wiley, 1936.

Busino, Giovanni. *Introduction a une Histoire de la Sociologie de Pareto.* Genève: Droz, 1968.

Bouglé, Celestin, et al. "L'Oeuvre Sociologique d'Emile Durkheim." *Europe.* 15 February 1930.

Bousquet, George H. *Pareto, le Savant et l'Homme.* Lausanne: Payot, 1960.

———. *Précis de Sociologie d'après Vilfredo Pareto.* Paris: Payot, 1925.

————. *Vilfredo Pareto: sa Vie et son Oeuvre*. Paris: Payot, 1928.

Chambliss, Rollin. *Social Thought*. New York: Dryden, 1954.

Cresson, André. *Auguste Comte: sa Vie, son Oeuvre*. Paris: Presses Universitaires, 1941.

Davy, Georges. "Emile Durkheim." *Revue de Métaphysique et de Morale* 85 and 86 (1918, 1920).

————. *Sociologues d'Hier et d'Aujourd'hui*. Paris: Félix Alcan, 1954.

Dumas, Georges. *Psychologie de deux Messies Positivistes: St. Simon et Auguste Comte*. Paris: Félix Alcan, 1905.

Duvignaud, Jean-Auger. *Durkheim: sa Vie, son Oeuvre*. Paris: Presses Universitaires, 1965.

Fletcher, Ronald. *Auguste Comte and the Making of Sociology*. London: Athlone, 1966.

Fromm, Erich. *Man for Himself*. New York: Fawcett, 1967.

————. *Marx's Concept of Man*. New York: Frederick Ungar, 1964.

Gelke, Charles. *Emile Durkheim's Contributions to Sociological Theory. Studies in History, Economics, and Political Law*. New York: Columbia University Press, 1915.

Freund, Julien. *The Sociology of Max Weber*. New York: Vintage, 1969.

Giacalone-Monaco, Tommaso. *Pareto e Sorel: Riflessioni e Ricerche*. Pavia: Cedam, 1960.

Gouhier, Henri. *Auguste Comte: Oeuvres Choisies*. Paris: Aubier, 1943.

————. *La Jeunesse d'Auguste Comte et la Formation du Positivisme*. 3 Volumes. Paris: J. Vrin, 1933.

————. *La Vie d'Auguste Comte*. Paris: J. Vrin, 1965.

Gouldner, Alvin. *Enter Plato*. New York: Basic Books, 1965.

————. *The Coming Crisis in Western Sociology*. New York: Avon, 1970.

Halbwachs, Maurice. "La Doctrine d'Emile Durkheim," *Revue Philosophique* 85 (1918).

Honigsheim, Paul. *On Max Weber*. New York: Free Press, 1968.

Hughes, Stuart. *Consciousness and Society*. New York: Vintage, 1961.

Jaspers, Karl. *Three Essays*. New York: Harcourt, Brace & World, 1968.

Levy-Bruhl, Lucien. *La Philosophie d'Auguste Comte*. Paris: Félix Alcan, 1921.

Lopreato, Joseph. *Vilfredo Pareto*. New York: Crowell, 1965.

Manuel, Frank. *The Prophets of Paris*. New York: Harper & Row, Harper Torchbooks, 1965.

Mannheim, Karl. *Ideology and Utopia*. New York: Harvest, 1936.

Meisel, James. *Pareto and Mosca*. Englewood Cliffs, N.J.: Prentice Hall, 1965.

Meyers, Jacob P. *Max Weber and German Politics*. London: Farber & Farber, 1944.

Mill, John S. *Auguste Comte and Positivism*. Ann Arbor, University of Michigan Press, 1961.

Miller, S.M. *Max Weber*. New York: Crowell, 1964.

Mitzman, Arthur. *The Iron Cage*. New York: Knopf, 1970.

Nisbet, Robert. *Emile Durkheim*. Englewood Cliffs, N.J.: Prentice Hall, 1965.

————. *The Sociological Tradition*. New York: Random House, 1969.

Parsons, Talcott. *Essays in Sociology.* New York: Free Press, 1964.

———. *The Structure of Social Action.* Vol. 3. Glencoe, Ill.: Free Press, 1961.

Parsons, Talcott, et. al. "Max Weber Today," *International Social Science Journal* 17 (1965).

Pécault, Félix. "Auguste Comte et Durkheim." *Revue de Métaphysique et de Morale* 28 (1921).

Progoff, Ira. *The Death and Rebirth of Psychology.* New York: Julian, 1956.

Robinet, Dr. *Notice sur l'Oeuvre et la Vie d'Auguste Comte.* Paris: Dunod, 1860.

Shumpeter, Joseph. *Ten Great Economists from Marx to Keynes.* New York: Oxford University Press, 1951.

Sokoloff, Boris. *Auguste Comte, The Mad Philosopher.* New York: Random House, 1954.

Sorokin, Pitrim. *Contemporary Sociological Theories.* New York: Harper & Row, Harper Torchbooks, 1964.

Stark, Werner, "The Agony of Righteousness," *Thought* 63 (1968).

———. *The Fundamental Forms of Social Thought.* New York: Fordham University Press, 1963.

———. *The Sociology of Knowledge.* London: Routledge and Kegan Paul, 1958.

Thérive, André. *Clothilde de Vaux ou la Déesse Morte.* Paris: A. Michel, 1957.

Vialatoux, Joseph. *De Durkheim à Bergson.* Paris: Bloud & Gay, 1939.

Vine, Margaret. *An Introduction to Sociological Theory.* New York: David McKay, 1959.

Weber, Marianne. *Max Weber: Ein Lebensbild.* Heidelberg: Lambert-Schneider, 1950.

Weinreich, Marcel. *Max Weber: l'Homme et le Savant.* Paris: Librairie Philosophique, 1938.

Wolff, Kurt, *Essays on Sociology and Philosophy.* New York: Harper & Row, Harper Torchbooks, 1960.

Wrong, Dennis. *Max Weber.* Englewood Cliffs, N.J.: Prentice Hall, 1970.

Vilfredo Pareto: L'Economista e il Sociologo. Milano: Rudolfo Malfasi, 1955.

INDEX

Alpert, Harry, 56

Altruism, 26, 28, 35; potentialities for, 37; preponderance of, over egoism, 39; subordination of egoism to, 29, 31, 146

Analysis, of social theories and thought, 3, 11. *See also* Theory(ies), Thought

Anthropology, 11, 78

Aristotle, 20, 44, 49, 54

Aron, Raymond, 112

Art, as means of expression, 45

Assumption(s), central, of humanistic tradition, 2; four basic sets of interrelated, 8-11; identification of, about man and society, 4; of what man is, 8; of what society is, 8; on biography of man and society, 9; on conception of ideal man, 5, 142; on the essence of sociology, 9-11; panideological, 6. *See also* Ideal man, Man, Society, Sociology

Astronomy, 33

Authoritarianism, German, 111

Bakunin, Allessandrina, 85

Baumgarten, Hermann, 117, 130, 131

Baumgarten, Ida, 117

Bazard, Saint-Amand, 15, 16

Behavior, and emotions, unified, 37, 145; human 9; irrational, Pareto on, 100

Belief, axiological, metaphysical, 4. *See also* Metaphysics

Bergson, Henri, 4, 76, 81, 82, 127

Bichat, Marie François Xavier, 26

Biology, differentiation between sociology and, 47; methods and results of, 26; positive theory of human nature in, 29; subordination to sociology, 26. *See also* Positivism, Sociology

Biopsychic, and social man, Comte on, 147; animal, man seen as, 91; being, 56-57; organism, 2, 145. *See also* Man

Bismarck, Otto von, 40

"Body physical," 30

"Body social," 30

Bonald, Louis Gabriel Ambroise de, 15, 17

Bouglé, Célestin, 53

Bousquet, George, 84

Boutroux, Etienne Emile Marie, 64, 148

Brain, 25, 27, 34, 36. *See also* Harmony

Brotherhood, 117

Busino, Giovanni, 84, 158